Patrick T. Quinn

**Money in the garden**

A vegetable manual, prepared with a view to economy and profit

Patrick T. Quinn

**Money in the garden**

*A vegetable manual, prepared with a view to economy and profit*

ISBN/EAN: 9783744735803

Printed in Europe, USA, Canada, Australia, Japan

Cover: Foto ©Lupo / pixelio.de

More available books at **www.hansebooks.com**

# MONEY IN THE GARDEN.

---

A VEGETABLE MANUAL,

PREPARED WITH A VIEW TO

ECONOMY AND PROFIT,

BY P. T. QUINN.

PRACTICAL HORTICULTURIST.
AUTHOR OF "PEAR CULTURE FOR PROFIT."

---

NEW YORK:
ORANGE JUDD COMPANY,
1906

# CONTENTS.

## CHAPTER I.

|  | PAGE |
|---|---|
| MONEY IN THE GARDEN | 13 |
| Location and Selection of Soil | 14 |
| Draining | 14 |
| Preparing the Ground | 16 |
| Manures | 18 |
| Capital | 20 |

## CHAPTER II.

|  |  |
|---|---|
| HOT-BEDS | 22 |
| Straw Mats | 26 |
| Cold Frames | 28 |

## CHAPTER III.

|  |  |
|---|---|
| ARTICHOKE | 32 |
| Asparagus | 34 |
| Sowing the Seed | 37 |
| Preparing the Ground | 38 |
| Planting | 39 |
| Varieties | 44 |
| Cutting and Bunching | 45 |
| Profits | 48 |
| Insects | 49 |

## CHAPTER IV.

| | PAGE |
|---|---|
| Beans | 52 |
|    China | 53 |
|    White Kidney | 53 |
|    Pole-Beans | 55 |
| Beets | 59 |
| Borecole | 64 |
| Broccoli | 68 |

## CHAPTER V.

| | |
|---|---|
| Cabbages | 72 |
| Carrots | 97 |
| Cardoon | 108 |
| Cauliflower | 109 |
| Celery | 111 |
| Celeriac | 125 |
| Corn Salad, or Fetticus | 127 |
| Cress, or Peppergrass | 127 |
| Water-Cress | 128 |
| Chives, or Cives | 129 |
| Chervil | 130 |
| Chervil, Turnip-rooted | 131 |
| Corn | 131 |
| Cucumbers | 135 |

## CHAPTER VI.

| | |
|---|---|
| Egg Plants | 142 |
| Endive | 148 |
| Garlic | 150 |
| Horse-Radish | 151 |
| Kohl-Rabi | 155 |

## CHAPTER VII.

| | |
|---|---|
| Lettuce | 159 |
| Leek | 163 |
| Martynia | 166 |

## CHAPTER VIII.

|  | PAGE |
|---|---|
| MELONS | 167 |
| Melon, Water | 170 |
| Mustard | 172 |
| Mushrooms | 172 |
| Nasturtium, or Indian Cress | 177 |

## CHAPTER IX.

| ONIONS | 179 |
|---|---|
| Okra, or Gumbo | 187 |

## CHAPTER X.

| PARSLEY | 189 |
|---|---|
| Parsnip | 192 |
| Peas | 194 |
| Peppers | 198 |
| Potatoes | 200 |
| Jerusalem Artichoke | 214 |
| Pumpkins | 215 |

## CHAPTER XI.

| RADISHES | 217 |
|---|---|
| Rhubarb | 221 |

## CHAPTER XII.

| SALSIFY, OR VEGETABLE OYSTER | 224 |
|---|---|
| Scorzonera | 225 |
| Sea Kale | 225 |
| Spinach | 226 |
| New Zealand Spinach | 229 |
| Shallots | 229 |
| Sorrel | 230 |
| Squash | 230 |
| Sweet Potatoes | 233 |

## CHAPTER XIII.

|  | PAGE |
|---|---|
| Tomatoes | 237 |
| Turnips | 244 |
| Herbs | 252 |

## CHAPTER XIV.

| | |
|---|---|
| Forcing-houses for Vegetables | 254 |

## CHAPTER XV.

| | |
|---|---|
| A List of Seeds for the Kitchen-Garden | 263 |
| List of Plants | 264 |
| Quantity of Seed to an Acre | 267 |
| Vitality of Garden-Seed | 267 |
| Distance Table | 268 |

# PREFACE.

Now-a-days a non-literary practical man, if tolerably successful in any special'y, must do one of two things. He either must keep his own counsel and reticently go on, making what profit he may, or he must be prepared daily to answer a thousand-and-one questions by mouth, and by letter, conscious that his "pursley" is getting ahead of him, while he casts and recasts multitudinous counsels from his one little mould of experience.

There *is* a way of evading these alternatives, though it may call for a radical change in the nature of the aforesaid practical man. He can go into a book, there say whatever he has to say, and, going out again (backward at the preface), explain humbly: friends, you will find it all in this volume. I've been as matter-of-fact and explicit as possible, avoiding speculation, and putting down, briefly, things I have learned from daily toil and the wisdom of other men.

This is why these two hundred and sixty-eight pages of simple and conscientious directions are given to all who, by saving or gaining, hope to find "MONEY IN THE GARDEN."

P. T. Q.

NEWARK, N. J., March 1, 1871.

# MONEY IN THE GARDEN.

## CHAPTER I.

IN this work the author aims to give, in a plain, practical style, instructions on three distinct, although closely connected, branches of gardening—the kitchen-garden, market-garden, and field culture of root-crops—the only credentials for the fitness of his undertaking being a successful practical experience for a term of years.

Modern gardening simply is another term for improved methods of farming, and success either in the kitchen or market-garden, depends upon carrying out these methods.

At present, no thinking cultivator can overlook the need of a more general use of the best labor-saving implements. Land is plenty. Manure, in most sections, can be obtained at home, or bought at reasonable rates. The last ten years have been exceptional in the high prices of farm and garden produce. The only drawback to a relative profit has been the high price of farm-labor.

This can only be overcome by a more extended use of improved tools in preparing the ground, planting the seed, cultivating and harvesting the crops. Such implements as have been used, and found of real value, are described or referred to under their proper headings.

## LOCATION AND SELECTION OF SOIL.

These are important points, both for the kitchen and market-garden; in regard to the latter, proximity to the market is among the first considerations. As a large quantity of horse-manure must be carted every year from the city or town, and all kinds of garden-stuff must be delivered to the commission-men or hucksters, which is most economically done with the producer's own team, it follows that a favorable location within a few miles of a good market increases the chances of success.

Garden vegetables, as a rule, will thrive best, other things being equal, on a deep, sandy loam, with an open sub-soil. Almost any character of soil, with the exception of pure clay, can be brought up to a high state of fertility by adopting the proper methods; but, as in gardening, "the early bird catches the worm," and a week's difference in the time of ripening often makes a difference of from one to two hundred dollars in the gross receipts from an acre, the sandy loam will have the advantage over a heavy clay soil, even if they are equal in other respects.

DRAINING.—The garden soil should be deep, thoroughly pulverized, and free from stagnant water. Many soils are well adapted to the growth of vegetables, and require no draining. But where the

ground is kept cold late in the Spring, from the
effects of stagnant water or surface springs, it is
useless to attempt the cultivation of such land, *with
a view to profit,* until it is thoroughly drained. We
have never known of an instance, when a judicious
outlay having been made for draining soils of this
character, but the result, in a
few years, has fully justified
the expenditure by vastly increased productiveness, with
the same amount of labor and
manure that, before the land
was drained, would barely
pay expenses.

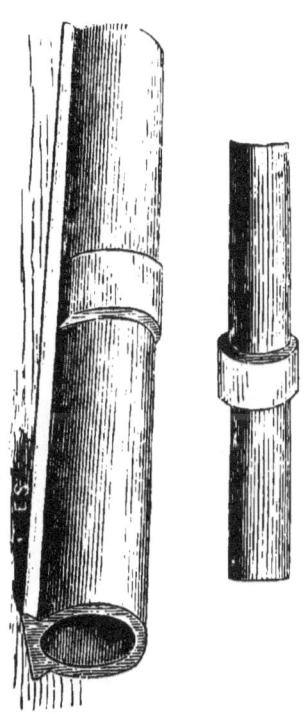

DRAIN TILES.

The cost of draining an
acre of ground will depend
to some extent on the price
of labor, the tenacity of the
soil, and the price of the tiles
or other material that will answer the same purpose.

In case the soil is com-
pact, the drains should be
twenty feet apart and three
feet deep; with a more por-
ous sub-soil, thirty feet between will be close enough.
Stones are frequently used for this purpose, but, even
when in abundance on the land, they will be found
the most expensive and least effectual. Round pipes,
or sole tiles with collars, when properly laid, best answer the purpose. Next to these, hemlock boards

## PREPARING THE GROUND.

"ripped" in the centre, lengthwise, and then nailed together in the form of the letter ∧, will, when laid on a firm bottom, with enough fall, outlast a generation. The expense of tiles or boards is about the same—one and three-quarter cents a foot. To avoid making a blunder in so important a matter, it is always best to employ an engineer to run the lines and mark the levels. Twenty-five dollars so spent will never be regretted. The expense, counting everything, usually amounts to fifty or sixty dollars an acre. When the sub-soil plough is used to loosen the soil before digging the drains, the cost may be very materially lessened.

PREPARING THE GROUND.—A soil having an average depth of four or five inches cannot be brought up to the standard of excellence in less than three

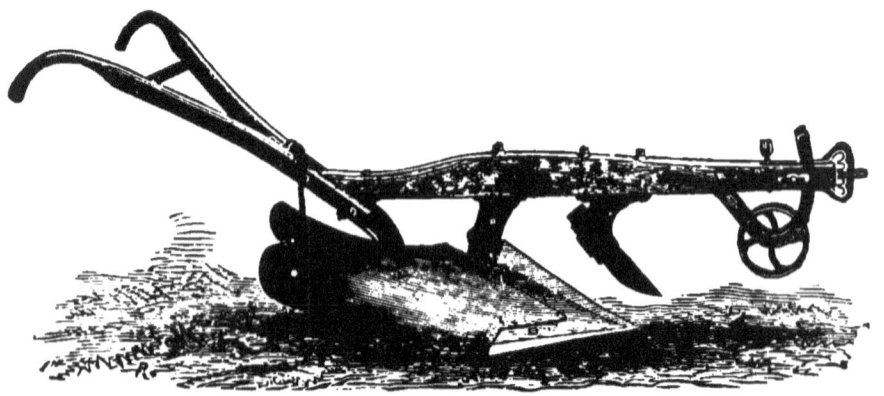

HOLBROOK'S SWIVEL PLOUGH.

years. The first step to be taken is to deepen it; this is partly done by surface-ploughing eight or ten inches deep, in the Fall, and following, in the bottom of the furrow, with a lifting sub-soil plough. The ground should be ploughed in ridges ten or twelve feet wide, with deep, open furrows. This treatment will leave the soil in the best condition to be acted upon by the frost. In the kitchen-garden the deepening will have to be done with the spade and digging-fork.

In the Spring, the ground is harrowed down, a heavy dressing of well-rotted manure spread broadcast, and ploughed under. The more manure applied, the better will be the crop the first year.

MAPES' LIFTING SUB-SOIL PLOUGH.

A crop of Potatoes planted on this soil the first season, will be found one of the best. The cultivator and hand-hoes should be kept active during the early stages of growth, so as to subdue the surface-soil.

In the Fall, when the Potatoes have been dug, another application of manure, forty or fifty loads to the acre, the ground is again ploughed, and then Spinach may be put in, giving in addition a dressing of three or four hundred pounds to the acre of finely-

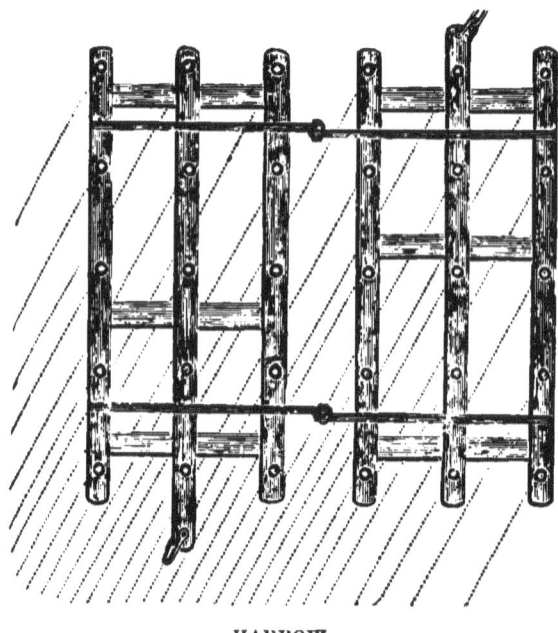

HARROW.

ground bone or superphosphate of lime. This brings us to the important subject of

MANURES.—No matter how favorable the location, nor what the character of the soil may be, he tills to great disadvantage who fails to make a liberal annual application of manures. The question for the gardener is, How much manure can I use with increased profit? and, if he is alive to his own interest, he will soon discover that the quantity that can be so applied to an acre is large.

Of the bulky manures, that from stables where

the horses are fed on grain and hay is of most value. This quality of manure, almost free from straw, we buy at Newark, N. J., at an average of one dollar and thirty-eight cents for a two-horse load. This is hauled and thrown in heaps, sometimes composted with tanner's refuse and woods earth, turning it over two or three times before applying it.

Market-gardeners will use from fifty to seventy loads of this manure to an acre, besides a top-dressing of five or six hundred pounds of a special fertilizer.

For the past four years we have contracted for all the refuse from a large soap factory, and have found this waste lime, potash, and fatty matter a valuable top-dressing, applying it at the rate of three or four tons to the acre. We have also used a compost made by decomposing muck with the salt and lime mixture,* then adding to this compound an equal bulk of yard-manure. At the end of six months the whole mass is homogeneous, and, when turned under for garden-crops, fully equal, load for load, to pure horse-manure.

Gardeners in our section use "slaughter-house" manure with profitable results. This is usually composted with other manures, and left in a pile for several months before using it. It costs about one dollar and fifty cents a two-horse load, and in quality is about the same as a load of horse-manure.

* The salt and lime mixture is made by dissolving one bushel of salt in water, and then slacking three bushels of lime with the salt water. This mixture should be turned over two or three times under a shed; one bushel of it will be enough for a cord of muck.

We have used as much as seventy-five tons of dried blood, or sugar-house scum, in a single season; when this is broken finely, and composted with horse-manure and woods earth, it is a powerful fertilizer for all kinds of crops.

Wood-ashes are always highly esteemed, but of late years the supply has been very limited. Unleached wood-ashes are worth from forty to fifty cents per bushel; for fertilizing purposes, using ten to twenty bushels to an acre. A top-dressing of lime every third year, thirty or forty bushels to the acre, spread broadcast, and harrowed in just before planting, pays handsomely.

Every available substance that will make manure should find its way to the compost heap or hog-pen, to be worked over, and thus add to the capital for the garden; on this will greatly depend the success.

Of the concentrated fertilizers now in general use, both for the kitchen and market-gardens, are finely-ground bone, Peruvian guano, superphosphate of lime, and last, but not least in value, fish guano. The required quantity of these will depend on the condition of the soil. Besides the main supply of yard-manure, we use annually from three hundred to one thousand pounds to an acre, and find that such an application of a pure article pays well.

CAPITAL.—With the farmer, the laying out of a kitchen-garden should be of the first consideration. In spare moments a fence can be put around the garden, which should be located convenient to the dwelling. With a full supply of the leading kinds of vegetables, farmers could board their help for about one-half of what it costs when only meat, bread, and Potatoes form the principal food. With the farm-work properly arranged, the kitchen-garden can be kept in good order without any extra cost for labor.

For the market-gardener, capital is very important when the proprietor knows how to use it—an art learned only by experience.

It does not make much difference how intelligent a man may be in other respects, nor how much capital he has to start with; if he has had no experience in the business, he lacks the main element of success.

We know personally a large number of well-to-do market-gardeners—men now worth from ten to forty thousand dollars each—none of whom had five hundred dollars to begin with. Industrious, hard-working men, these, who at first turned every available dollar into manure and reliable seeds. In fact, he who would be successful in market-gardening must take the lead in all kinds of weather and all kinds of work—late and early, rain or shine. To stalwart young men, even with a limited capital, willing to begin in a small way and work industriously, the chances of making " money in the garden" are as promising as ever they were. 'Whatever is done, let it be well done."

# CHAPTER II.

## HOT-BEDS.

*Location.*—Select a southeastern exposure, protected from the north wind by a board-fence, hedge, or the side of a building. Then excavate the ground eighteen inches deep, eight feet wide, and as long as required, allowing three feet for each sash.

*Making the Bed.*—Gardeners in the latitude of New York start their hot-beds from the 1st to the 15th of February. When started early, more manure is used, so that enough bottom-heat may be supplied to keep the young plants growing until mild weather sets in. Commence by putting a layer of cold horse-manure, six or eight inches in thickness, on the excavated surface. Begin at one end of the intended bed, and be careful that this first layer, as well as all succeeding ones, is spread evenly. Then add a second layer of hot manure, of about the same thickness as the first. The mass may now be trodden down by walking on top of it, keeping the feet close together. Another layer of hot manure may then be put on, the frames placed in position, and pressed down firmly. Add another layer of fine manure, ten or twelve inches in thickness, inside of the frames, as a finish, and put on the sashes.

The beds being eight feet wide, and the frames

only six, there will be a margin of twelve to sixteen inches outside, which should be banked up with manure as high as the top of the frame.

*Frames* may be made of common boards nailed together, with a post in each corner for a support. They should be five feet ten inches wide from front to rear, and as long as desired—the front board twelve inches high, and the rear eighteen to twenty-four. The frames, when made, should stand level on the bottom, forming an inclined plane on top; so that, when the sashes are on, there will be enough fall from rear to front to cast the water readily.

*Cross-ties* six feet long, made of narrow strips of boards, one by three inches, should be mortised into the front and rear boards of the frames every three feet. These will support the sashes and strengthen the frames.

*Sashes* can be bought from any sash manufacturer. They should be well constructed of seasoned wood; if not, the heat of the beds will warp the wood, displace and break the glass. The narrow lights of glass, 4 x 6, are preferable. These should be cut curved on the lower edge, so that the water will run off in the middle of the light in single drops, and not form lenses, which would likely scorch the plants.

*Putting on Earth and Sowing Seed.*—When the beds are finished, as stated before, the sashes are put on at once and covered with straw mats. In case the weather is pleasant, the mats may be taken off for three or four hours the next day. Two days from the time of making, under ordinary circumstances, the earth may be put on. This should not be done, however, until the manure is well heated inside the frames. Six or eight inches of leaf-mold, or good garden-soil free from stones, will answer.

Two or three days from the time of putting in the earth the seed may be sown. Select a pleasant day, and remove all the sashes and mats. Unless the soil is very rich, a handful of bone-flour or superphosphate should be sprinkled over each light. Then turn the earth over with a digging-fork, and rake the surface level; for, if left slanting, the frequent watering will wash the seed from the upper or rear part of the bed.

Make shallow drills from rear to front two inches apart and about three-quarters of an inch deep; sow the seed in these drills, and cover lightly by sifting earth over the bed until the surface is again level. Each kind of seed should be sown separately, and labeled at the time of sowing. Replace the sashes, and, toward night, put on the mats. Except in very cold weather, the mats should be taken off daily about 9 or 10 o'clock in the morning.

The secret in growing strong, stocky plants is, when they are well up, to give an abundance of air at the right time. For instance, if the sashes are opened soon after removing the mats, the chances are that the young plants will be injured by what gardeners call "damping off." While the plants are young, no air should be admitted into the beds for at least one hour after the mats have been removed. Each succeeding mild day more air may be given to the plants, to keep them from growing spindling.

# HOT-BEDS.

Egg-plants and Peppers require more heat and less air than Cabbages, Cauliflowers, Tomatoes, or Lettuce.

When Tomato plants are two inches high, they should be pricked out into another frame. Those who make a business of growing Tomatoes in a large way, for market, transplant them twice before setting them out in the field. Each time that they are moved from one bed to another, more room is given in order to get short, stocky plants.

Egg-plants will do better, producing more fruit, and earlier, if transplanted or put into "thumb-pots," and placed in beds made like a hot-bed, only using less manure.

The beds should be watered with tepid water when the surface becomes dry. In April the plants will require water every day.

WATERING POT.

There are few neighborhoods where enough plants cannot be sold to more than pay the expenses of making and caring for the bed. When the young plants are taken from the seed-bed, Cucumbers and Melons can be started under the glass, and transplanted to the open air in May. These plants will produce fruit two weeks before seed planted in the open ground.

## STRAW MATS.

Every gardener who grows early vegetables must have a supply of straw mats to cover the sashes, when forcing vegetables or plants by bottom-heat. These mats are made at odd times during the Winter, when nothing more important is on hand. At our farm we have a wooden frame, made of four boards nailed together. This frame is eight feet long and five feet wide. In the centre of the top board there are five nails fastened about ten inches apart, and five more on the bottom board, to correspond with the upper row of nails or pegs. Before commencing with the straw, five pieces of marling or tarred twine are cut about twenty-eight feet long; one end of each piece is fastened to a nail on the top board, then drawn tight and fastened to the corresponding lower nail. The surplus twine is wound around short pieces of green wood, with a slit in one end to keep the twine from unwinding. Sound rye straw that has been thrashed with the flail is the best kind for making mats. They will be made more quickly if the straw has been arranged beforehand, shaking out some of the short or broken pieces, and getting the butt-ends of the sheaves even.

When everything is in readiness, two men or boys stand in front of the frame, having a sheaf of straw close to the edge of the frame on either side.

# STRAW MATS. 27

Each takes a small quantity of straw and places it on the lower board resting on the nails, the butt-ends

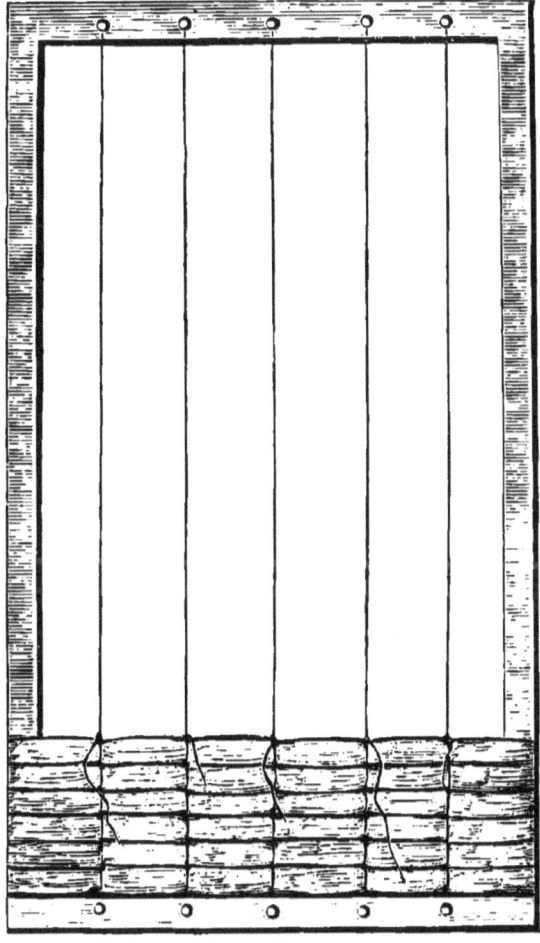

MAT FRAME.

of the straw toward the outer edge of the frame. Then, while holding the straw in position with the left hand, with a quick movement, each in turn of the five sticks is taken around the upright twine, and the straw made fast by a slip-knot. This is repeated until the top row of pegs is reached, when the mat is finished. Some gardeners use seven pieces of twine, and state that the mats last twice as long as when made with five. Two expert men or boys accustomed to the work will make eight mats a day, working nine hours.

These mats will be found useful for many things, as well as protecting hot-beds from frost; they will last much longer if rolled up and placed under cover when not needed out of doors.

## COLD FRAMES.

These frames may be constructed of rough hemlock boards, placing them two deep in the rear of the bed, and only one in front.

When a suitable situation has been chosen, the length of the frame should be north and south, so that the beds will secure the advantage of the morning sun. The width or distance between the rear and front boards of the frame should be five feet ten inches, and the length as necessity may demand. The top of the frame, when properly made, should be eight or ten inches above the level of the adjoining surface, and the top board of the rear of the frame about two inches higher than the front one; so that, when the sash is placed in position, there will be enough fall from rear to front to readily carry off the water. The boards are nailed fast to posts driven well into the ground, one at either end of the boards, and one in the middle, to strengthen the frame.

## COLD FRAMES.

Every three feet narrow strips or cross-ties should be neatly mortised in the rear and front boards, and then nailed in position. These give more strength, and also make a support for the sides of each sash when the plants need covering. Cold frames differ from forcing-beds only in having no bottom-heat.

The soil should be a good quality of garden-soil, and at least twelve inches deep. Before transplanting, this soil should be well forked over, making it fine and mellow, and then raking the surface level. From five to eight hundred plants may be set under each sash of 3 x 6. If the weather is warm at the time of transplanting, it may be well to shade the plants for a few hours in the middle of the day. In case the plants are more than three inches high, when transplanting them, to prevent their growing any more during the Fall, it is better to remove the sashes from the frames every mild day, until such time as the cold weather sets in.

Cold frame plants require but little attention during the Winter months; an occasional airing on mild days will be quite sufficient. This can be done by raising the rear or side of each sash, and placing a support under it for three or four hours in the middle of the day. During very cold weather this is not necessary, nor does it at all injure the plants to be frozen. The gardener's care is to prevent, if possible, the too frequent alternations of freezing and thawing brought about by the sudden changes through the Winter. As the weather grows milder, approaching Spring, the plants should have plenty of air every day. Within comparatively few years market-gardeners situated near large cities have turned their attention to growing Lettuce under glass, and they find it a profitable business.

Large quantities of frame-lettuce are now annually grown near New York, in frames similar to those described for Cabbage and Tomato plants. The only difference being, that they must be more carefully constructed, and the soil should be of better quality than that used for plants.

About the 1st of November the Lettuce plants are transplanted into the frames, putting not more than fifty plants to each sash. When planted closer than this they seldom form large heads, and have to be sold as "basket-lettuce," instead of so much per head, which makes quite a difference in the receipts. Lettuce planted in cold frames in November will be salable in April, and will generally sell readily at from three to five dollars per hundred. Gardeners usually make two dollars per sash on Lettuce raised in this way, and the demand is always good when the Lettuce is well-grown and carefully put up. With bottom-heat, a crop is ready for market in nine weeks from the date of planting.

For Lettuce-growing, the "span frame" is becoming popular among gardeners near New York. It is similar in its construction to the ordinary frame, only it is double, instead of single. A piece of joist is placed along the centre, supported by posts driven into the ground; then cross-ties are mortised into this joist every three feet on either side, and then into the front boards. This will make the bed nearly twelve feet wide, instead of six, being higher in the centre—enough to give a good fall for the water when the sashes are placed on the frames. A frame arranged in this way will, with the same kind of treatment, produce more full-grown heads of Lettuce to the sash than the ordinary single frames in common use among gardeners.

# CHAPTER III.

### ARTICHOKE.

*Cynara scolymus.*

THERE are only two varieties of this vegetable that are grown in the gardens of this country—the common green, and green globe. The latter is of better quality, and gives more edible part in proportion to the bulk of the heads than the common kind.

The Artichoke is propagated from seed, or by suckers, when the plants are once established. The seed should be sown in a moderate hot-bed about the 1st to the 10th of March, and, with proper care, the plants will be large and strong enough to transplant into the open ground by the 1st of May. They are rank feeders, and succeed best when planted in an open situation, in a deep, rich loam. Unless the weather is very moist when they are transplanted, they should be freely watered for a week or two after having been set out.

Suckers from the old plants should be taken off early in April, keeping as much of the fibrous roots as possible with the detached plants. Before planting they must be carefully trimmed, removing all the outside leaves. Plants put out in the Spring, 3 x 3, will produce heads in July, and continue to do so until the 1st of November. As soon as the head

ARTICHOKE. 33

is taken off, the foot-stalk should be cut down close to the main stock or root.

GREEN GLOBE ARTICHOKE.

As far north as New York the Artichoke needs protection during the Winter. We have saved ours for a number of years in the following manner:

Early in December the old leaves are removed carefully, so as not to injure the main stock; then, by a digging-fork, some mould is thrown from either side of the row towards the row of plants, raising a mound of earth covering part of the plants. Then a coating of leaves or long manure, five or six inches deep, is put on top of this earth and along the line of plants.

Early in April this covering is removed, levelling the earth from around the plants before the young sprouts start. If wanted for a new bed, then these plants can be transplanted, as described above. Not more than three shoots should be allowed to a hill. Some gardeners rub off every alternate bud, so as to increase the size of those left on.

In this part of the country the culture of the Artichoke is principally confined to private gardens; it is seldom found in the northern markets. But in California it is extensively cultivated, and it may be found on the tables, served as a vegetable in all the first-class hotels and restaurants.

## ASPARAGUS.

### *Asparagus officinalis.*

The Asparagus is a hardy perennial, that, under proper management, when planted in the right kind of soil, will produce annual crops for an indefinite length of time. When well-grown and carefully bunched it is sure to meet with a ready sale. The demand for it has always been good, even when other vegetables were dull and selling at low prices. From year to year one hears the same question asked by the consumers of Asparagus, Why is it that this vegetable is not more generally cultivated? The area devoted to its culture has been increased very much, but not enough to keep pace with the likewise growing demand.

During the last twenty years I have been engaged, more or less each year, in raising vegetables for market, and, at different times I have known each and every kind of vegetable, grown to any extent for market, become a "drug," with the single exception of Asparagus, which, thus far, has always been in good demand, and that, too, at paying prices.

There are few persons who have been engaged on an extensive scale in "trucking," who have not been compelled, in "bad seasons," to sell a part or the whole of a crop for less money than it cost to produce it. This would apply to the whole list of vegetables, leaving out Asparagus, which, during such dull seasons and poor markets, is generally made use of by those who grow it to work off other kinds of vegetables—that is, in case a grocer wants two or more dozen of Asparagus; to get it he would be obliged to buy a portion of whatever the grower had in his wagon at the time. In this way the gardener who had an abundance of Asparagus would not lose as much in the sale of his crops in dull seasons as he who was not so situated.

Within the past ten years more attention has been given to the culture of Asparagus. It is not rare, now, to find fields of from two to seven acres, in different sections, devoted to Asparagus for the New York and other large markets. Some of these new plantations have already begun to yield well, and yet prices are not in the least affected; on the contrary, they have advanced. Growers estimated the yield, during the past season, to have been above an average one, and still prices ranged higher than they have for many years. This condition of matters is quite encouraging for those who have young beds, or are about to embark in this branch of gardening with a view to profit.

To be successful in the culture of Asparagus for market there are a few essential points to be fully considered and carried out before any reasonable hopes of success can be entertained.

The first is a selection of the most suitable soil and situation; the second, a thorough mechanical preparation of the soil before planting, and the third, heavy manuring.

The location of the bed is highly important. When Asparagus first comes into market it sells briskly at from five to eight dollars per dozen bunches, and frequently as high as twelve dollars per dozen, if the spears are large and the bunches carefully made. From these prices it gradually falls, as the supply increases, until it reaches two dollars per dozen. Below this price it very seldom goes, although at one dollar and fifty cents per dozen Asparagus will pay a handsome profit.

When the soil has only been indifferently prepared and poorly manured, earliness of the crop and large-sized spears cannot be expected, and, as a matter of course, under such circumstances, large profits are not realized by the producer.

### SOWING THE SEED.

Asparagus-seed should be sown in the Spring in a bed made deep, mellow, and rich. When the surface of such a bed has been raked over, removing any stones or other obstructions, shallow drills should be opened, about one inch deep and a foot apart. The seed must be strewed thinly, by hand, in these drills, and then covered by raking the bed with wooden rakes, drawing them in the direction of the drills. In favorable weather fresh seed will sprout in two weeks from the time of sowing. Seed older than one year will take longer to germinate, and, if more than three years old, it is unsafe to sow it; there is no prospect of its ever germinating. In case the seed is older than one year, soaking it in milk twenty-four hours before sowing will cause it to germinate sooner.

It is a good plan to scatter some Radish-seed in the drills at the time of sowing the Asparagus-seed. The Radish will germinate and come up in a few days from the time of sowing, marking the lines of the rows. This will give a chance to run a scuffle-hoe between the rows, destroying any weeds that may have appeared, and keeping the surface loose until the Asparagus plants are well up. Then the spaces between the rows should be disturbed frequently, and no weeds or grass allowed to grow. Well-grown one-year-old plants will be strong enough for transplanting into the permanent bed. If the plants are weak, it is better to let them remain in the seed-bed another season. Plants older than two years should not be set out ; it is more than probable they will fail to give satisfactory results.

Those who want only a few hundred plants, to make a family bed, will find it cheaper to buy them from some responsible person than to attempt to raise them from the seed. One pound of good fresh seed will sow a bed 20 x 100 feet, and give from twelve to fifteen thousand plants.

### PREPARING THE GROUND.

Asparagus will succeed best on a deep, sandy loam, that is rich and mellow. There should be no short-sighted economy practised in preparing the ground for an Asparagus-bed. All the outlay for labor and manure, judiciously laid out in making the bed, will be returned to the owner, with a high rate of interest, within the next ten years.

If the ground selected is naturally wet, or likely to become so, then by all means have it thoroughly underdrained. Asparagus can only be grown to the highest point of profit on soil that is free from stagnant water, thoroughly pulverized to a depth of at least twenty to twenty-two inches, and then heavily manured. There will be more satisfaction from planting only a quarter of an acre on this thorough scale, than in planting an acre under indifferent preparation and poor manuring. The ground should be thoroughly ploughed and sub-soiled both ways, and then plenty of well-rotted yard-manure ploughed under. The more manure that is applied, the more

ASPARAGUS. 39

productive the yield will be when the plants are fairly established. Barn-yard manure, composted with the *salt and lime mixture*, will be found an excellent manure for Asparagus.

In garden-culture the ground selected should be forked over to the same depth, and plenty of manure added before planting. Ground in "good heart," with an application of from forty to fifty two-horse loads of manure to the acre, will produce paying crops. A dressing of fifteen or twenty bushels of salt to the acre, before setting the plants, will be found of service.

### PLANTING.

It has long been a mooted question whether the Fall or Spring is the best time to plant an Asparagus-bed. In most cases more will depend on the condition and tilth of the soil than on the time of setting out the roots. Where the soil is heavy and retentive of moisture, and the Winters long and severe, undoubtedly the Spring is the best time. But on sandy or clay loam, and as far south as Delaware or Virginia, Fall-planting will do just as well, and often better than Spring-planting, under similar circumstances.

When the ground has been prepared by frequent ploughings and sub-soilings for field-culture, or the garden-spot thoroughly trenched with the spade or digging-fork, then open furrows ten or twelve inches deep, four feet apart one way and two feet the other. When the bottoms of the furrows are levelled, they should not be more than nine inches deep. A single

# ASPARAGUS.

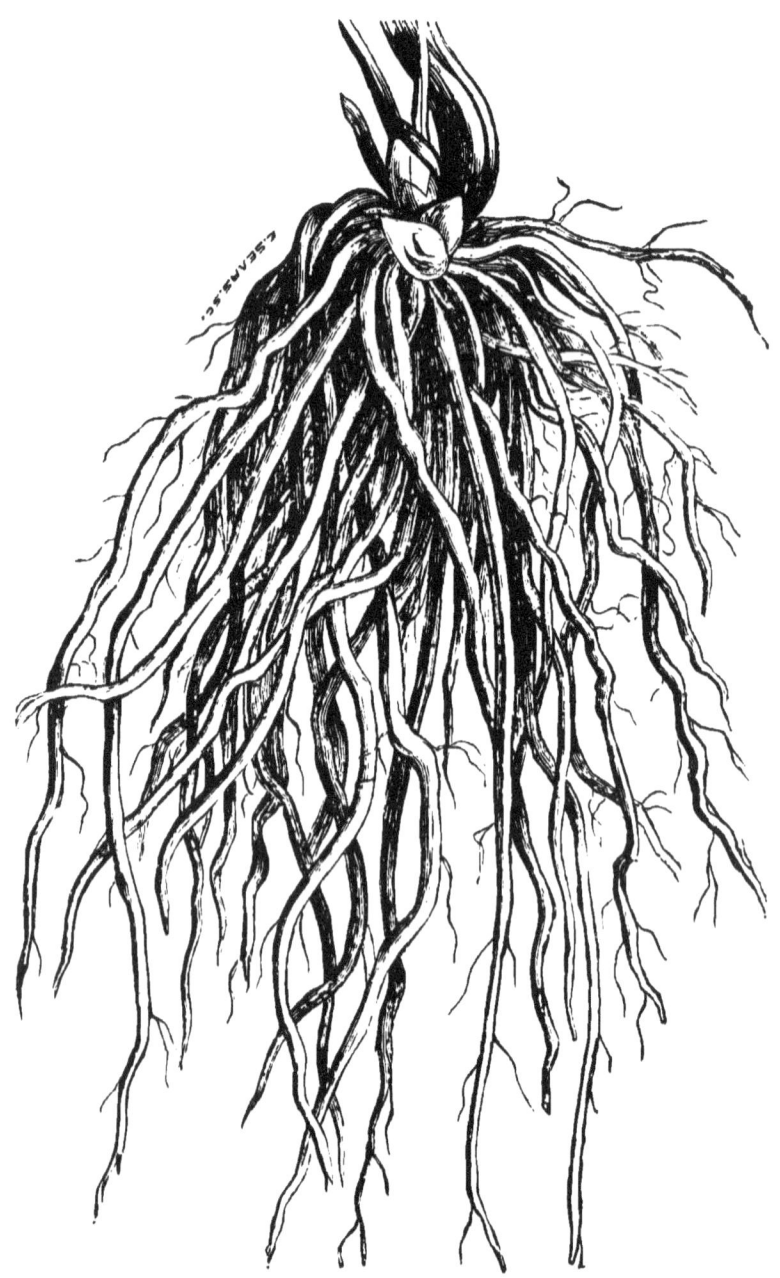

ASPARAGUS ROOT.

plant is set at each intersection, care being taken that each root of the plant is drawn out horizontally to its full length. At this distance apart there will be about five thousand five hundred plants to an acre, and two hundred plants will be abundant to supply a family of six persons. When set out in the Spring, the crowns of the plants should not be covered more than three inches. This light covering at first, or until the plants have started to grow, is the safest plan to follow. When the young shoots are three or four inches above the surface, run a cultivator between the rows; the loose earth will fall towards the plants, adding a few more inches of covering above the crowns, so that, by the end of the first Summer, the surface will be quite level.

When the Asparagus is planted in the Fall, the plants will have to be covered full depth at once; if not, they will be in some danger from the snow and water settling over the crowns, and then freezing.

In garden-culture the second covering may be drawn over the roots by the hand-hoe any time during the Summer. A cultivator should be kept going between the rows often enough to prevent the growth of weeds in the bed. This will be found the cheapest method of culture. When planted in the Fall, the rows should have a light mulch of barn-yard manure put on in November and in the Spring following; this mulch, with an additional quantity of manure, either barn-yard, fish, guano, bone-dust, or superphosphate, should be turned under early in April, or as soon as the ground is dry enough to be worked.

Annual dressings of common salt will improve the quality and increase the size of Asparagus. There need be no apprehension of danger from the application of salt. I have frequently put on as much as two inches in thickness on different parts of an Asparagus-bed, and the young plants have come through this coating of salt without any apparent injury. A dressing of twenty-five or thirty bushels of salt to the acre, every second year, will be quite enough, in connection with the annual covering of barn-yard manure or compost to be applied in the Fall or Spring, as circumstances may dictate.

No Asparagus should be cut from the bed the first or second year. Some growers go so far as not to cut any until the fourth year from the time of planting. If the plants have grown vigorously, a crop may be cut without at all injuring the plantation the third year. The amount that may safely be taken off at this time depends altogether on the condition and vigor of the plants. In case they are weak, it would be poor policy to weaken them still more by cutting for market or home consumption too soon.

In the Fall of the first year it is a good plan to throw shallow furrows from either side towards the rows, and then round them off with a hoe or rake. This slightly-elevated ridge will dry out sooner in the Spring than a flat surface; and Asparagus, treated in this way, will often make a difference in earliness of five or six days, which is an important item to those who grow it for market.

Early Asparagus always brings a much higher

# ASPARAGUS.

price than that which comes in late in the season. Therefore every advantage from location, character of soil and treatment, must be taken into consideration by those who cultivate for profit.

When the plants are set so that they have about nine inches of covering at the end of the third year from the time of planting, the crowns will be within seven inches of the surface. At this depth the beds may be ploughed with a one-horse plough in the Spring, and the spaces between the rows kept clean by a cultivator during the rest of the season. In garden-culture the "crowns" need only be covered four or five inches. This will save considerable in the labor of working an Asparagus-bed over the old method of digging the whole surface every Spring, and doing most of the work with the hand-hoe during the Summer.

CONOVER'S COLOSSAL.

## VARIETIES.

ASPARAGUS KNIFE.

Until quite recently there were only two varieties generally cultivated for market purposes—the green and the purple-topped. The identity of these two has been frequently maintained by many intelligent gardeners, who attribute the differences in size and color to location, soil, and heavy or light manuring. There is no doubt in my mind about these two being distinct varieties, and that they will show their peculiarities when grown on the same ground and under the same treatment. With heavy manuring the size can be increased very decidedly, but high culture does not change the color of either.

Two years ago S. B. Conover, of New York, introduced a new variety of Asparagus under the name of "Conover's Colossal." For this variety Mr. Conover claimed superior qualities to either of the two varieties known and cultivated by market-gardeners. The spears of this variety were said to be of extraordinary size, of tender and good quality when cooked, and, for field or garden-culture, equally if not more productive than the green or purple-topped varieties. This claim had to be substantiated by practical growers before discarding old and tried kinds for new and untried ones. Many doubted its

ASPARAGUS. 45

being any other than what was cultivated on Long Island and in other Asparagus-producing sections.

I have for two years experimented with the "Colossal," and I am fully convinced that it is a new variety here, possessing many characteristics that will make it a valuable acquisition to our list of vegetables. Plants only one year old will average larger than plants two years old, of the other varieties, when grown on the same soil and under the same treatment.

Formerly, in making an Asparagus-bed, the plants were set too near together. With the "Colossal," 4 x 2 will be found better than close planting. Even with the green or purple-top, 3 x 2 will be found, at the end of five years, to produce more to the acre than if set nine inches in the row and eighteen inches between the rows.

CUTTING AND BUNCHING.

Cutting Asparagus intelligently is one of the nice jobs in gardening that cannot, without careful instructions, be delegated to Tom, Dick, or Harry. A careless use of the knife often spoils more stocks just under the surface than there are spears fit for use above.

The time to cut is before the head of the Asparagus branches out and loses its compact form, when the spears are from six to eight inches long. The knife must be kept sharp. It should be of a certain shape, as seen on p. 44. The blade of this knife is broad, and about eight inches long; most of the cutting has to be done with the point of the knife. It should be run down, almost perpendicularly, alongside of the spear, cutting the spear obliquely about two inches below the surface. By this method very few, if any, of the young shoots are injured by the point of the knife. When the bed is three years old, or the third year from the time of planting, it may

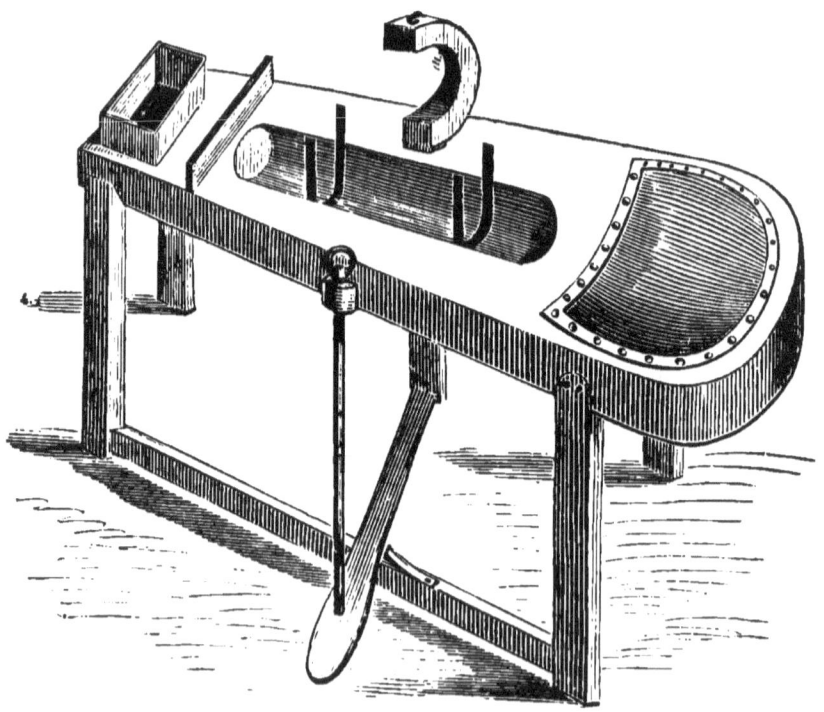

BUNCHING MACHINE.

be cut regularly each year. Not later, however, than the middle of June, in the Northern States. After this date the spears should be allowed to run to seed.

Where Asparagus is cultivated for market, bunching and tying are another part of the business that requires skill and practice. The bunches, to look well, must be of uniform size and length. Almost every grower has, for bunching, a contrivance of his own invention; some of these are very primitive. The best that I have seen is represented on p. 46. It is simple in its construction, and does the work well. A man of ordinary intelligence can make one of them in a couple of hours. It is two and a half feet high, three feet long, and eighteen or twenty inches wide on top. It looks on top like a saddler's work-bench without the jaws. In front of the seat there is a place hollowed out, with two narrow pieces of iron hoops fastened the proper distance apart, and curved, so as to give the right shape to each bunch. Before putting the spears of Asparagus in place, two tying-strings of the right length are laid across this mould. When the bunch is large enough, the hinged top-piece is brought down and the loop from the treadle placed on the side-button or hook, then by the right foot the treadle is pressed down and fastened in an iron slot. The bunch is then tied with bass-matting or narrow strips of the bark of water elm. The treadle is then loosened, the bunch taken out, and the operation repeated. A thin piece of board is put across in front of the first piece of iron, so that, in bunching, all the heads of the Asparagus may be pressed against this board. The butt-ends are cut off all the same length the day on which they are sent to market.

Sometimes a grower cannot send the Asparagus to market every day, but he is compelled to keep it for three or four days. By placing the bunches in pure cold water, and then covering them, they may be kept four or five days, and when taken out they will look as fresh as if just cut. Or if, when cut, before bunching, the spears are thrown on the cellar-floor, and, when bunched, placed in cold water for a few hours, each spear will swell out and look fresh. The box on the front of the machine is intended for keeping a knife, strings, &c., &c. By winding the string around the box, when the string is cut in one place it will be the right length for tying the bunch.

A few years ago white Asparagus was in demand but lately there has been little call for it. However, any one can have white Asparagus by keeping the light away from it while growing. This can be most cheaply done by covering the bed thickly, about the 1st of April, with a coating of salt hay or long manure, eight or ten inches deep.

Before cutting the Asparagus the litter is moved one side and then replaced.

### PROFITS.

The annual returns from an acre of Asparagus depend so much on the character of the soil and the treatment it receives that it is difficult to state the exact amount. Some growers, favorably located, make from six to seven hundred dollars a year profit. This is much more than is realized by most growers. Taking one year with another, a well-kept Asparagus-bed will yield four hundred and fifty dollars per acre profit.

Since the close of the late war large plantations of Asparagus have been made in certain localities of the Southern States. This Asparagus will find its way to the Northern markets, and, owing to the natural advantages of climate, its early appearance will affect the profits of Northern growers. Asparagus can be shipped from Southern ports with but little risk of injury, even if several days should elapse before it reaches its destination. Open crates the same kind as those now used by Peach-growers will answer for shipping Asparagus to Northern markets.

## INSECTS.

Within the last ten years Asparagus-growers have had serious cause for alarm, by the introduction of an insect from Europe. The *Crioceris asparagi* has been doing a great deal of damage on Long Island and in the Asparagus-producing districts of New Jersey. This insect made its appearance about 1860. Since that time it has multiplied so fast, that, unless some effectual means is discovered to check its ravages, Asparagus-growing will be rendered unprofitable in some localities where now it is grown on a large scale.

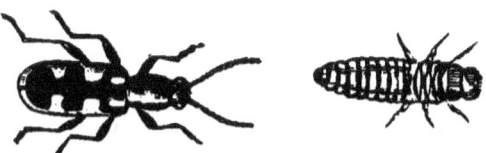

BEETLE AND LARVA.

The eggs of this insect are oblong. They are placed on the plant by one end, one egg being sometimes attached to the end of another. They hatch in about eight days. The larva is very slow in its movements, and feeds on Asparagus, eating holes through the bark; when disturbed it ejects a noisome liquid from its mouth, and does much injury to the plant. The pupæ are formed under fallen leaves and rubbish on the earth. The insect appears in about thirty days from the period of laying the egg; it hibernates under the bark of trees, moss, lichens, old rails, &c., &c. As stated, it came from Europe, and made its first appearance on Long Island.

The best remedy that is yet known is to dust the plants with fresh air-slacked lime on beds one and two years planted. On young beds the insects do most damage. With bearing-beds, by allowing the thin shoots to remain uncut, the larva collects on them and does not injure the larger saleable spears. By going through the bed once a day with a basin of hot water, thousands can be shaken into the water and are destroyed. This will, in many cases, check their depredations. Fine bone-meal has been tried by some growers with satisfactory results. This dusting can only be done with young beds, or thin spears on old beds; for, if put on spears intended for table-use, the Asparagus will taste of the lime or bone. The thin shoots can be cut off occasionally, and burned, destroying what are collected on them.

Forcing.—When Asparagus is wanted before the out-door beds produce in April, it can easily be brought forward in hot-beds or forcing-pits. For this purpose old roots are required; those from six to ten years old are the best.

The roots should be put into the bed in February, and covered with about three or four inches of earth.

## ASPARAGUS.

From seventy-five to one hundred plants may be set in a light of 3 x 6; when they start to grow this number of roots will yield from fifty to sixty spears a day. The temperature should be kept above sixty degrees, and on mild days the bed should be copiously watered and aired. It should be covered with straw mats at night to protect against frost. In very cold weather a bank of horse-manure, placed around the outside of the frame, will help to keep the temperature up to at least sixty.

# CHAPTER IV

### BEANS.

*Phaseolus vulgaris, &c.*

Of the Dwarf, Kidney, or Snap Beans there are many varieties, but only a few are in general cultivation.

Formerly this variety of Bean was extensively raised by market-gardeners on Long Island, and in parts of New Jersey, for the New York market; but since the close of the late war the principal supply, early in the season, comes from Virginia and South Carolina, where labor and land are cheaper than they are in the neighborhood of Northern cities.

The most popular and profitable varieties of the Snap Bean for field or garden-culture are the following:

Early Valentine.
Refugee, or Thousand to One.
Early Mohawk.
Wax.
White Kidney.
China.

The Early Valentine is decidedly the most profitable to plant for home use or market. This variety will ripen ten or twelve days before any of the others, though planted at the same time and under the same treatment. This difference in date of ripening often makes an increase of fifty dollars in the market receipts.

The Valentine is a tender Bean, of good quality, and very productive.

The Refugee, or Thousand to One, is not so early as the Valentine, but it answers well to follow as a second crop, if planted at the same time. For many years I planted it as a late variety for pickling, but the Early Valentine has taken its place, and I now like it better than the Refugee for this purpose.

The Early Mohawk is a late Bean, larger, and more hardy than the other varieties. The pods are long, very tender, and of good quality.

The Wax Bean is of comparatively recent introduction, and, for family use, is a great favorite. The pods are large, tender, of superior quality, and remain green and fit for table use longer than any other kind on the list.

CHINA.—At one time this variety was considered valuable for market, but, when planted alongside of the Early Valentine, the latter will be found the more profitable. The China is said to be a few days earlier than the Valentine, but I have grown them side by side many a time, and have always found the Valentine fit to gather first. When young, the pods of the China are very tender and sweet, but they soon turn yellow and hard.

WHITE KIDNEY.—This is a large, late variety, and, on account of its color, it is preferred for drying for Winter use. In a green state, the pods are not as tender nor of as good a quality as the other varieties.

The Kidney Dwarf Beans are not very hardy. If planted before settled weather, there is danger of their rotting in the ground, or of their being injured by late frosts.

It is safe to plant Snap Beans any time from the 5th to the 20th of May, in the latitude of New York, for the first planting. For garden-culture, a succession of plantings should be made every three weeks until September, so the table may be constantly supplied with young Beans all through the season.

These Beans will succeed best on a rich, sandy loam. drills open about three inches deep and two feet apart, for field-culture. The seed is then scattered thinly along these drills, about an inch apart. It takes five pecks to seed an acre. The seeds may be covered by a one-horse plough, a common hand-hoe, or by drawing the soil over them with the feet. The cultivation is principally done with horse-tools; a mule and Carrot-weeder will do all that is necessary to keep the surface loose and the weeds down; or going over them once with the hand-hoe will be quite sufficient.

The product per acre varies from seventy-five to one hundred and fifteen bushels of green Beans, and they usually bring from two to four dollars per bushel for the early crop in the New York market. When they do well, they will generally pay a profit of about one hundred to one hundred and fifty dollars per acre, one year with another.

String Beans carry very well. Two years ago my brothers shipped from Charleston, South Carolina, over five hundred bushels, during the season, to New York, without having a bushel damaged on the way.

For Southern planting, the Early Valentine has given the most satisfaction to gardeners for its earliness, productiveness, and good quality. When this variety is scarce and cannot be had, the Refugee, or Thousand to One, is the second choice, but in no instance has it been as profitable as the Early Valentine.

For garden-culture, where the cultivation is done with hand-tools, the rows need not be more than fifteen or eighteen inches apart, according to the quality of the ground. On poor soil the rows may be closer together than when the soil is in good heart.

In general, Southern growers have not been careful enough in packing Beans for the Northern market. At the time of packing, every Bean should be green. A single over-ripe pod will frequently spoil the sale of a whole crate.

### POLE-BEANS.

Although there are many varieties of the Pole or Running Bean, but few of them are cultivated with profit. The White Lima and the Horticultural Cranberry are the only kinds commonly found in market. Occasionally some of the other varieties are grown in private gardens, but very seldom by American gardeners.

The following is a list of some of the best sorts for garden or field-culture:

Large White Lima.
Dutch Case-Knife.

Horticultural Cranberry.

The Running or Pole Beans are not so hardy as the Snap Beans. In the latitude of New York they should not be planted in the open ground before the middle of May. With a wet, cold Spring, Lima Beans frequently rot if planted early, and sometimes the gardener is obliged to plant them over three different times before he can get a set of plants.

Pole Beans will succeed best on a deep, rich, sandy loam that has been thoroughly worked before putting in the seed. When grown for market, earliness has always to be taken into consideration, and, to forward the ripening, many methods have been practised by wide-awake gardeners. Some plant the Beans in moderate hot-beds, in April, and by this means get plants two or three inches high by the middle of May. Other gardeners adopt a more simple and practical method. Inverted sod is placed in the cellar, then cut into small squares, and a single Bean planted in each square. When the weather is settled, the sods with the growing Beans are planted around the hills. Where this plan is carried out, all risk of the Beans rotting is avoided, and there will be a difference of two weeks in the date of ripening.

When ready for planting, the ground is marked out four feet each way. At each intersection a hole twelve inches deep is made with a crowbar, and a cedar pole is set firmly in each of these holes. A forkful of well-rotted manure should be placed around each pole, and covered with about two or three inches of fine soil, making a hill around the pole two inches higher than the surrounding surface,

BEANS. 57

and fifteen inches in diameter. A circular drill is opened on this hill about an inch deep. Six Beans are planted, at equal distances apart, in this drill, always placing the eye of the Bean downward. This is an important fact to bear in mind, as the Lima Bean rises from the ground in this position. When the Beans are in position, a light covering of fine soil should be drawn over them.

One quart of Lima Beans will plant about three hundred hills, allowing six or seven Beans to each hill. The same quantity of the Case-Knife or of the Horticultural Cranberry will plant a hundred hills more, owing to their being a smaller-sized Bean. It is always best to use fresh seed; that which was grown the previous season is preferable, although Beans two years old will germinate.

When the young plants are two or three inches above ground they should be thinned out, leaving only three plants to a hill. In field-culture, the working between the rows is done by horse-tools; running the cultivator both ways leaves very little to be done with the hand-hoe. When the vines are two feet long, it is best to go through the patch and fasten up those that are not inclined to twine around the poles. The Lima Bean always winds around the pole in the same direction; that is, from west to east, or in the apparent opposite direction from the movement of the sun.

When the vines are six feet high the ends should be pinched off. This will cause them to throw out long side-shoots, that will yield a bountiful supply of large pods, hanging within easy reach for gathering.

The profit from the culture of Lima Beans varies, from year to year, according to the season and the supply in market. When grown on ground well prepared, and near a home-market, two hundred dollars per acre above expenses may be realized. I have frequently gathered, on an average, one quart of dry Beans from a pole. They usually sell from four to six dollars per bushel, and are always in good demand. From eighty to ninety bushels to the acre of dry Lima Beans is considered a good yield, and they seldom sell for less than four dollars per bushel. There is very little difference in the profit whether the Beans are sold green or dried.

Running Beans require a strong soil, and it is useless to attempt to grow them, with a view to profit, on thin, poor soil. Well-rotted hog-pen manure, applied in the way described, will give a fine growth of Beans. A small quantity of finely-ground bones, or of superphosphate, applied to the hill at the time of planting, or at the first hoeing, gives the young plants a vigorous start, which they are likely to maintain through the whole season.

The first outlay in preparing to grow Beans is for good, heavy poles. Cedar are the best; they will cost from one to three dollars per hundred; but if they are put under cover during the Winter, they will last eight or ten years.

The size and productiveness of Running Beans may be increased from year to year by selecting for seed only the largest pods, and, from these, saving none but the finest specimen beans.

## BEET.

*Beta vulgaris.*

The Beet is a rank feeder, and only produces maximum crops with heavy manuring and high culture. It is one of the leading and most profitable early crops grown by market-gardeners near large cities. When the ground has been well prepared and the seed fresh, the crop seldom fails.

The varieties most generally cultivated, either for market or home use, are the following, named in the order of their value for market:

E. B. T.

EARLY BLOOD-TURNIP.—This is the most popular early variety now cultivated by gardeners. It grows rapidly, and, when of full size, is tender and of good quality.

DARK RED EGYPTIAN TURNIP BEET—This is a new variety, that is highly spoken of by those who grew it last year. It is said to be ten or twelve days earlier than the Blood Turnip, and, in quality, fully equal to that variety.

EARLY FLAT BASSANO.—This is an excellent Beet, a little coarser in texture than the Blood Turnip. It does not sell as well in market, owing to the rings in the flesh of the Beet being alternately white and red.

This is not pleasing to the eye, and therefore injures it for a market variety. The Bassano is a favorite in the kitchen-garden for home consumption, and is very early.

LONG SMOOTH BLOOD BEET.—This is without doubt the most popular Long Beet, either for market or family use. When grown on strong ground, the roots are long, smooth, free from rootlets, and of fine quality.

The WHITE SUGAR and MANGEL WURTZEL are grown as a field-crop in dairy districts, and they deserve a passing word in that connection.

DARK RED EGYPTIAN BEET.

When Beets are grown for market, the ground is heavily manured early in the Spring, using fifty to seventy tons of yard-manure to the acre. This manure is ploughed under, the surface levelled, and then the ground marked out, the rows fifteen to eighteen inches apart, with a garden-marker. The seed is put in with a seed-drill, using four to six pounds of fresh seed to an acre. Four pounds would be quite enough, provided all the seed would germinate and come up. But it is always better to have garden-seeds come up too *thick* than too *thin* ; especially is it so with Beets, for, when young, they will sell readily by the barrel for greens. Gardeners sometimes sell from thirty to forty dollars worth from an acre of Beets when thinning them out. In case the seed-drill does not cover the seed sufficiently, passing along the rows and drawing the earth by the feet over the seeds will secure a full covering.

It is a good plan to sow some Turnip or long scarlet Radish-seed in the drill at the same time. The Radishes mature, they are pulled and marketed before the Beets are of any size.

Those sown early will be ready for market in June, and the crop all off by the 15th of July. When pulled, the Beets must be trimmed, removing all the decayed leaves and the rootlets, then washed and bunched, putting four or five beets to each bunch. This is considerable trouble, but they usually bring from seventy-five cents to one dollar per dozen bunches, and, with a good crop, they will yield about two hundred and fifty dollars an acre profit. In some favorable localities the profits will average higher, but in our garden the sum named is the amount generally realized. During the growing-season the ground must be kept loose, and free from weeds. The young Beets must be thinned out to three or four in-

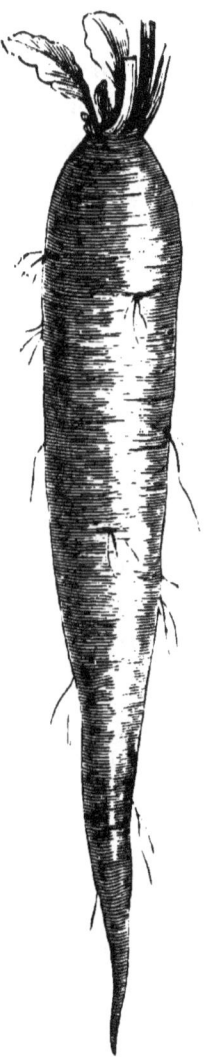

LONG SMOOTH BEET.

ches apart in the row when the plants are about three inches high.

The Blood Turnip will mature sooner than the Long Smooth Blood, and a larger space is devoted to its culture by practical gardeners, who sow it in the Spring for market. For Winter use, the seed may be sown as late as the 15th of June; in fact, the Beets from seed sown at that time will be found more tender in the Winter than those from seed sown earlier. The same is true of the Long Blood Beet. The latter is more popular for market, as well as for table use, during the Winter and Spring months.

The White Sugar and Mangel Wurtzel are generally cultivated as field-crops for feeding stock in the Winter. When grown for this purpose, the distance between the rows should be from two to two and a half feet, so that the cultivation can be done with horse-tools, instead of with hand-hoes.

Ground that is in good heart, and well worked by ploughing, harrowing, &c., &c., will yield from twenty to twenty-five tons of Beet-root to the acre, with an application of fifteen or twenty two-horse loads of yard-manure.

When everything is ready, the surface should be raised into narrow ridges; that is, with a one-horse plough, commencing at one side of the field, two furrows should be thrown together. A continuous system of back-furrowing is what is wanted. The tops of these ridges are then raked off with an iron rake or hoe, removing any stones, lumps, &c., &c.

The seed may be sown from the 1st to the 15th

of May with a seed-drill, using five or six pounds of seed for an acre. As soon as the plants are well up, a horse-tool should be passed between the rows, disturbing the surface, so that the weeds may gain no headway while the plants are small. By sowing the seed on these ridges, instead of on the level, the cultivator may begin at once without injury to the

ROOT CLEANER OR CARROT WEEDER.

young plants. The soil loosened by the cultivator will fall to the centre of the furrow between the ridges, and not on the young beets.

By running the root-cleaner between the rows once every two weeks, the weeds may be kept down without trouble and at a trifling cost.

When three inches high, they should be thinned out to five inches apart in the rows. Later in the season the Beet-tops give so much shade, that little culture will be required to keep the field perfectly free from weeds. The important point is to gain time early in the season; for, if the weeds once get ahead, it is hard work to get the best of them.

The culture of the different kinds of roots for stock-feeding is destined, before long, to form a large branch of farm-industry, and they can be grown at a moderate expense when labor-saving implements are introduced in their cultivation.

Roots grown for market or for cattle can be kept all Winter in root-cellars, or in pits out of doors. Full directions for making and covering such pits will be found under the head of Carrots, in another part of this book.

## BORECOLE.

*Brassica oleracea acephalo.*

We have of Borecole, as well as of many other kinds of vegetables, a long list of varieties, but comparatively few of them are cultivated either in private gardens or for market. Among those that are grown to some extent are the following:

BRUSSELS SPROUTS.—This variety is generally cultivated in private gardens. It grows from two to four feet high, and produces miniature Cabbages from one to two inches in diameter all around the stem. These small compact heads are the parts preferred for cooking. The top of the plant resembles a half-grown head of Savoy. These top leaves are sometimes used as greens in Winter; they become quite tender when touched by the frost.

The seed of the Brussels Sprouts may be sown in April in the open ground, and the plants put out in the garden in June, two and a half feet apart each way. They should be cultivated in the same manner as late Cabbages. If transplanted in June, they will be fit for use in September, and will continue to produce until checked by frost. If some of the late planting are "lifted" before the cold weather sets in, and "heeled in," covering the roots and part

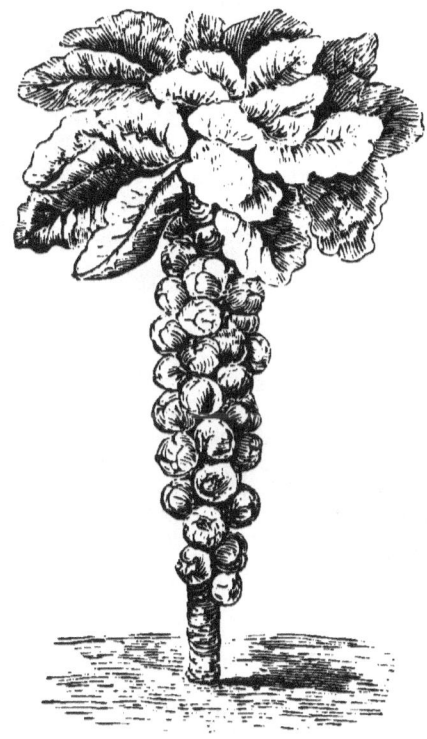

BRUSSELS SPROUTS.

of the stem with earth, in a cellar, they can be used during the Winter months; they will be found delicate in flavor, and tender.

This variety should be planted in a deep, rich

soil, and kept carefully cultivated while growing. When seed is wanted, select the best specimens late in the Fall, and give them the same care recommended for wintering seed Cabbages. Fifty plants will be enough to supply a medium-sized family with these miniature Cabbages.

DWARF GERMAN GREENS.—This hardy variety is well known to market-gardeners near New York,

GERMAN GREENS.

and is more generally grown than any other kind of greens. It is called "SPROUTS," and cultivated extensively on Long Island and in New Jersey for the

New York market. It will grow and winter better on a rich, sandy loam, than when raised on a heavy soil. The seed should be sown in September, using two pounds of seed to an acre, on ground well manured and worked, in rows, from twelve to fifteen inches apart. When the plants are two inches high, let them be carefully hoed, thinning them out where they are too thick. Some gardeners put on a mulch of salt marsh-hay in December, removing it in April. When the SPROUTS have made a fair growth in the Fall, mulching is not necessary. When Spinach is scarce, this kind of greens sells freely in large quantities and at very profitable rates. Where it does well, gardeners realize from two to three hundred dollars per acre profit. Prices often fall very low. I have known hundreds of barrels of Sprouts to be sold at fifty cents, and even less, per barrel, while other seasons they will range from two to four dollars per barrel. Two ounces of seed will yield enough for garden-culture for home use. The seed can be sown early in April, and tender greens can be had in this way in June. When grown on rich soil it is very tender. It is a favorite variety among the Germans for Spring greens.

GREEN CURLED SCOTCH.—This is another good variety, but not grown so extensively as the GERMAN GREENS. The seed of the SCOTCH should be sown in April and transplanted in June, the same distance apart, and treated the same as in the cultivation of Late Cabbages.

The ground should be kept well hoed or cultivated during the early part of the growth, because, later in the season, the leaves spread so as to prevent culture. The Green Curled Scotch Borecole is hardy, and improves in quality for table use when touched by frost. It will grow two feet high and two or three feet in diameter, when planted on good soil and carefully cultivated. It is grown in small lots for market, and is much liked by those who know anything about it. It is very desirable as a Winter vegetable.

PURPLE FRINGED.—This variety so nearly resembles the Scotch, except in its color, that there is nothing gained by cultivating the two in the same garden. In size, habits, and quality, they are similar, requiring the same kind of ground and treatment to bring them to maturity. One ounce of Borecole-seed will produce over four thousand plants. A small paper of the seed will give plants enough for the kitchen-garden.

## BROCCOLI.

*Brassica oleracea botrytis.*

There are a number of kinds of the Broccoli, all of them resembling the Cauliflower in form and growth, as well as in appearance and flavor of the edible part. As yet, the Broccoli is grown to a very limited extent in this country; this may be attributed to the uncertainty of the crop. In England, where the climate is more moist, it is a profitable crop among market-gardeners near London or other large cities. But, with us, practical gardeners are very cautious about risking too much in a single season, knowing from experience that a drought of three or four weeks' duration may destroy the whole crop. I have occasionally succeeded with Broccoli one season; then, being encouraged to plant on a larger scale, I have failed the following three, losing more than I made the one successful year.

When the crop does succeed, it pays a handsome profit. Well-formed heads seldom bring less than from twelve to fifteen dollars per hundred, or from one hundred and twenty to one hundred and fifty dollars per thousand, and always in brisk demand. The market is never over-stocked with Cauliflower or Broccoli.

For early Summer use the seed of the Broccoli may be sown in the open ground about the 1st to the 10th of September, and pricked out into cold frames in the latter part of October. Before cold weather these frames should be covered with sash, and the young plants receive the same treatment as that recommended for Early Cabbages. Early in April they may be transplanted into the open ground. They require a very rich, deep, and rather heavy soil. They should be set out in rows two feet and a half apart, and the plants two feet apart in the rows. The ground should be frequently hoed, preventing the appearance of weeds and grass. By the middle of June the heads will begin to form. If the weather is very warm, the heads sometimes "button," or run to seed. By bending some of the large leaves over the young heads, to shade them from the hot sun, the buttoning may be prevented.

For a Fall crop the seed should be sown about

the 1st of May, and transplanted into the garden or field early in July, setting them the same distance apart, and cultivating them in the same way as the Spring crop. With moist, cool weather in September and October, the Broccoli will head when planted on good soil. Besides the regular quantity of barnyard manure, an application, at the first hoeing, of three or four hundred pounds to the acre of Peruvian guano, will be found a good investment in growing Broccoli for profit.

There are only two varieties that are grown for market to any extent:

WHITE CAPE.—This is the most popular kind of Broccoli, and looks very much like Cauliflower, the only difference being that the heads are a creamy instead of a pure white.

PURPLE CAPE differs only in color from the WHITE CAPE. In other respects it is very similar; and when the plants are strong and healthy, they are of first quality, fully equal to any other sort that I have grown.

The seed of the Broccoli and Cauliflower is imported from England and France, as that grown in this country is not reliable. The young plants in the seed-bed are subject to the annoyance of the Cabbage-flea (*Haltica striolata*), which very often destroys all the plants in a few days. A recipe to prevent the *fleas* destroying the plants will be found under the head of Cabbage; as also some specifics for the prevention of "club-root," which affects Broccoli and Cauliflower as well as Cabbage.

One hundred plants, of either the White or Purple Cape Broccoli, will be enough for a supply for the kitchen-garden.

In the Southern States the seed of the Broccoli should be sown late in May and transplanted in September. They will continue to grow and form heads all Winter, and, with quick transportation, it would pay to send them to Northern markets early in the Spring.

# CHAPTER V.

### CABBAGE.

*Brassica oleracea capitata.*

This popular vegetable might, with a considerable degree of propriety, be included among the staples, for it is in almost as general use as the Potato, especially among the working classes. Every working-man who owns or tills a piece of ground, no matter how small, will devote part of it to a Cabbage-patch. In fact, no kitchen-garden is complete without its well-tended square of Cabbages, both for Summer and Winter use.

The culture of Cabbages for market has been steadily on the increase in localities contiguous to large cities. At the present time single growers in our neighborhood will plant more Cabbages for market than were planted in the whole township fifteen or twenty years ago. Yet, every careful cultivator finds an equally ready sale for his crop at paying prices. It is no longer a rare sight to see, in the vicinity of large cities, manufacturing towns, and mining districts, fields of five, eight, or ten acres exclusively devoted to Cabbages. Where there is a good market near by, the cultivation of Cabbages generally proves a profitable part of the gardener's business. But to make it so, requires certain conditions to be fulfilled on his part ; if these are neglected, it would be much wiser for him to let Cabbage-culture alone.

To insure success with Cabbages as a field-crop, the soil must be stirred deeply, well manured, and thoroughly pulverized before planting. On thin, shallow soil, no matter how much manure is used, the " run " of Cabbages will be from medium to small, with very few large, solid heads. Large, fine Cabbages are always in demand, even when small ones are a drug in the market. The Cabbage is a rank feeder, and requires a deep, rich soil to bring it to the highest point of profit.

The market-gardener usually confines his efforts to the cultivation of the early varieties. This crop is without doubt the more important to him, especially if he is so situated that he can always rely on a plentiful supply of barn-yard manure at a low price; for, unless the early Cabbage ground is deeply worked and heavily manured, the crop will fail to yield any profit. From ground rich enough for Cabbages, a crop of Lettuce and one of Celery can be taken in addition to the crop of Cabbages, the same year; these three crops, when they all succeed, will give a handsome profit on the amount of capital invested.

A sandy loam that is thoroughly drained, either naturally or by artificial means, will be found the best for this crop, other things being equal. Earliness and large, uniform-sized heads are the important points to be gained by the gardener in its successful cultivation.

The seed for early Cabbages should be sown in the Fall, in the latitude of New York, between the 1st and 15th of September, in the open ground. About the middle of October they will be large enough to prick in cold frames, putting from five to eight hundred to a sash of 3 x 6. The plants should be set deeply, covering nearly all the stem. When cold weather sets in the sashes must be put on, and

GARDEN MARKER.

the only care necessary during the Winter will be to give them air. In mild weather, and on the approach of Spring, remove the sashes from the frames, so as to "harden off" the plants before setting them in the field.

Early varieties can also be grown in hot-beds; started in February, and the young plants trans-

## CABBAGES. 75

planted into other beds in March. They will be large enough to set out in the garden in April.

More explicit directions will be found on this subject in the chapter on "Hot-beds."

Market-gardeners prefer cold frame plants for their main crop of early Cabbages. As early in April as the ground is in condition to be worked, the yard-manure is hauled on the field, using from sixty to seventy-five two-horse loads to the acre. This is spread broadcast, and ploughed under. The surface is then levelled by turning a harrow upside down and dragging it over the ground, so as not to displace the manure. The space is then marked out, the rows two feet apart. The plants are then set in the rows, eighteen inches apart, with the ordinary dibble. This can be done very rapidly by persons familiar with the work. A smart workman will transplant seven thousand in ten hours. Lettuce may then be planted between the rows of Cabbages, one foot apart in the rows. With this method all the work of cultivation has to be done with hand-hoes; and with Cabbage, as with all garden-crops, clean culture must be the rule.

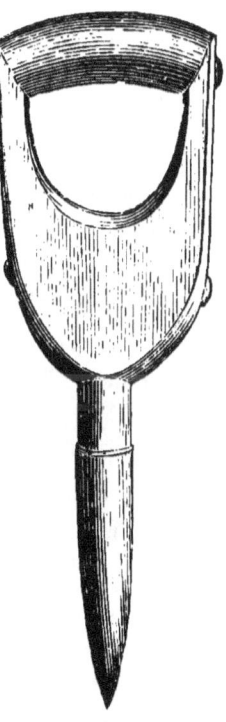

DIBBLE.

Farther south, where land is cheaper—as, for

instance, around Norfolk—a wider distance between the Cabbages, so as to use horse-tools, may be found advisable.

The Lettuce is cut and marketed in May, before the Cabbages need the room. They are ready for market early in July, and the whole is disposed of before the 20th, leaving full time for Celery. Besides the regular quantity of barn-yard manure, an application of three or four hundred pounds to the acre of Peruvian guano, finely-ground bone, or superphosphate of lime, scattered broadcast before planting, will be found of material use in perfecting the growth of the crop.

When planted at the distances named, there are usually about twelve thousand marketable heads. Of late years the average price has been sixty dollars per thousand, or seven hundred and twenty dollars per acre, from early Cabbages.

Practical gardeners calculate that the Lettuce and Celery will cover all the expenses, leaving the amount realized from the Cabbages as profit. Of course, the cost of yard-manure will affect the net proceeds. At Newark, N. J., or New York, a two-horse load of horse-manure, free from straw, costs only a dollar and a quarter or a dollar and a half. The same kind, at Philadelphia, will cost three times that amount. So that, as before stated, the profits will depend on the cost of manure, and the distance the same has to be carted, which will make a decided difference in the net result. There are a few special localities, near large cities, where manure can be had in abundance at low prices; in these places

# CABBAGES.

gardening can be carried on with more success and higher rates of profit than where manure is scarce and high, and produce has to be transported long distances.

There are only a few early varieties much cultivated by gardeners. The most popular of those now grown for the New York market is the

JERSEY WAKEFIELD.—The heads of this variety are large and solid, conical in form, and of a fine texture. With the same treatment, it will produce

JERSEY WAKEFIELD.

more marketable heads to the acre than any other early variety.

OXHEART.—This variety is still grown extensively for market, but it is not so reliable, nor so large, as the JERSEY WAKEFIELD. For the kitchen-garden, however, it is always a favorite and excellent kind.

LARGE YORK is grown to some extent, but it is every way inferior to the Wakefield and the Oxheart for market.

EARLY YORK.—This popular variety, better known and more generally cultivated than any other early Cabbage, has a small, compact head. Its earliness and delicate flavor have always made it a desirable sort for the kitchen-garden, but it is too small to be grown now by market-gardeners for profit.

EARLY FLAT DUTCH comes into market just at the close of the season of the early varieties, and usually sells for high prices. Our crop of this kind last year sold from twelve to fourteen dollars per hundred, with a brisk demand. The early Flat Dutch requires more room than the other varieties—at least two feet apart each way. We usually get about seven to eight thousand marketable heads from an acre.

EARLY WINNIGSTADT.—This kind is not as early on our farm as the early Flat Dutch, when planted on the same ground. Owing to its lateness in heading, it is not much grown for market by those who have cultivated the earlier sorts. But if a succession of varieties is wanted, it will serve to fill up a gap. It is of good quality, and boils tender.

LATE CABBAGES are grown in many localities on a very extensive scale, and the demand for large, solid heads is generally good, with prices high enough to leave a handsome margin for profit, when the expenses are deducted.

For the past ten years we have grown on our farm, near Newark, N. J., from seventy-five to one hundred and fifty thousand Fall Cabbages annually, and we find less trouble now in selling one hundred thousand heads than we did twenty years ago in disposing of one-fifth of that number. With a single exception, well-grown Fall or Winter Cabbages have not sold for less than sixty dollars per thousand since 1860. Frequently during that time they have sold freely at one hundred dollars per thousand, and even at higher prices. We have sold our crop the present

LARGE FLAT DUTCH.

Winter at one hundred dollars per thousand. But few varieties of Fall Cabbages are grown for profit by farmers or gardeners near New York. Among the best may be named the

LARGE FLAT DUTCH.—This variety has a large,

solid head, nearly flat on top, stem short, color pale green. It is the most profitable variety that we cultivate for Fall or Winter use. As it has but few outside leaves when the head is ripe, it does not winter as well as the Bergen with some growers.

LARGE LATE BERGEN.—The Bergen forms a large, rather round head, and very solid. It needs richer ground and more room than the Flat Dutch, as the leaves, when half-grown, are large and spreading. This variety should not be planted closer than two feet and a half each way; while the Flat Dutch may be the same distance between the rows, and only two feet apart in the row. Both kinds are of good quality.

STONE-MASON.—The Stone-Mason has a small, firm head, of good quality. In Northern localities it is not in any way superior to the early Flat Dutch, and it is too small to be grown for market.

DRUMHEAD SAVOY.—This variety is decidedly the best of the Savoys, either for market or the kitchen-garden. The head is large, solid, and the quality good. It is preferred by many to any other kind of Cabbage for Winter use. In planting, our custom is to plant one-eighth of the whole Savoys, and seven-eighths Flat Dutch.

GREEN GLOBE.—This is a small variety, only grown in the kitchen-garden. The head is small, the leaves quite wrinkled, and the color green.

RED DUTCH.—The demand for this variety is limited, as it is only used for pickling. It should be planted early in June, as it grows slowly, requires a long season to mature, and richer ground than the other Fall kinds.

# CABBAGES.

The culture of late varieties of Cabbage is quite different from the method described for the early kinds. Late Cabbages can be grown as a second crop, following early Potatoes, Peas, &c., &c., and the greater part of the cultivation can be done with horse instead of with hand-tools.

SOWING SEED.—Eight or ten years ago our rule was to sow the seed about the 10th of May, and

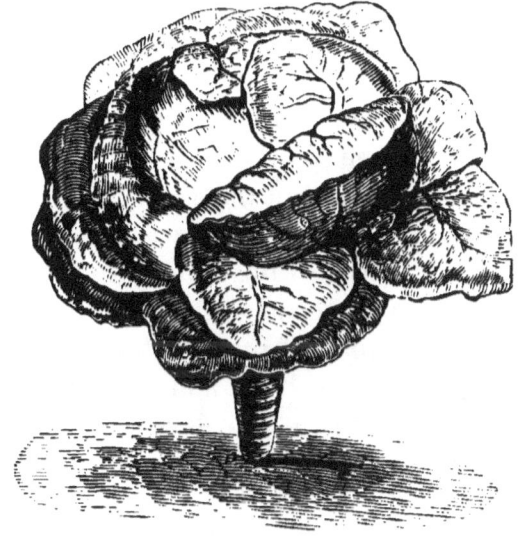

DRUMHEAD SAVOY.

finish planting before the 20th of July. But, for the last three or four years, late planting has not given satisfaction; a very large proportion of the plants set out after the 10th of July failed to make solid heads, being only fit for cow-feed in the Fall.

It is very important to the Cabbage-grower to have fresh seed, *true to name;* and every man who raises Cabbages as a field-crop should select, each year, from his growing crop, some of the best-formed heads to preserve for seed. The disappointment and loss from sowing impure seed are vexatious, and can only be avoided by following the above method. Before sowing, the seed-bed should be well pulverized and made rich by adding plenty of well-rotted manure, and forking it under, or by applying a liberal dose of finely-ground bone or superphosphate. The surface should then be raked level and smooth, removing any stones or hard lumps of soil. Then make shallow trenches, about one inch deep and one foot apart. The seed may be sown by hand in these trenches, endeavoring to sow evenly, by taking a small quantity of seed in the right hand and allowing it to pass into the trench between the thumb and fingers. Cover the seed by raking the surface of the bed lightly with a wooden rake, drawing the rake straight with the lines of the trenches.

When the seed is fresh and the weather favorable, it will come up in ten days from the time of sowing. At this stage of growth the young plants require close attention. If the weather is dry, the plants are frequently attacked by a small black insect (*Haltica striolata*) resembling a flea in appearance and deportment. I have known this little pest destroy one hundred thousand young plants in three or four days. In fact, if some measures are not instantly taken to stop his career, there will be but few plants left, no matter how much seed has been sown. Dusting the plants, when they first come through the surface, with flour of bone, and repeating it after each rain, will often keep them off.

## CABBAGES.

Another excellent remedy is to steep, at the time of sowing the seed, ten or twelve pounds of tobacco-stems in a large tub, adding three or four quarts of soft-soap and some urine. When the plants are up and any signs of the "fleas" appear, the bed may be syringed with this tobacco solution, and the plants dusted with some air-slacked lime. This should be done early in the morning, while the dew is on the plants. Two applications of this solution, followed by the lime, I have never known to fail in driving off these insects from the seed-bed.

During the early stages of growth, the spaces between the rows should be stirred frequently to keep down the weeds. The plants will do best on loose, mellow, fresh ground. One pound of fresh seed will give thirty to forty thousand plants, with careful treatment. Seed sown in good soil by the 1st of May will produce plants large enough to transplant into the field by the 10th of June.

Sowing a few seeds in the place where the Cabbages are to be grown, may do in the garden, but not in field-culture.

Late Cabbages, like the early varieties, require a deep, rich, and well-disturbed soil, free from stagnant water. A heavy clay loam, well fertilized, will bring a good crop of Fall Cabbages. On stubble-ground, intended for Cabbages the following year, we Fall-plough, throwing the ground into ten-feet ridges. This space is manured in the Spring and planted with Potatoes. Sometimes we adopt another method. In the latter part of April the ground is ploughed deeply, and during the month of May, when other important work is not pressing, we haul out, for Cabbages, from thirty to forty two-horse loads of compost or well-rotted barn-yard manure to the acre, according to the quality of the land. This is thrown in convenient-sized heaps, usually making four of a wagon-load, in regular lines and distances through the field. It is then spread broadcast, and ploughed under immediately.

Under ordinary circumstances, the soil, by this time, will be loose and mellow, and in fine condition for planting. Unless the ground is very rich, I generally apply a top-dressing, before harrowing the last time, of some special compost or concentrated manure, such as superphosphate, finely-ground bone, or fish guano, at the rate of from five hundred to one thousand pounds to the acre. In any case, the special manures are previously mixed with twice their own bulk of soil before application.

Cabbages will always do better, other conditions being equal, on a clover-sod, than on ground that has been previously cropped. On sod it is better to apply the long manure on the surface, and turn it under. Then top-dress the surface with enough of concentrated manure or compost, to give the plants a good start. The ground is marked both ways before planting, making the rows two feet and a half apart one way and two feet the other. This can be rapidly done with an instrument known to gardeners as a "marker." It is made of a piece of joist ten or twelve feet long, having holes bored every three inches, and a handle about six feet long mortised in the centre of the head, and braced from either side.

When completed, it looks like a hand hay-rake on a large scale.

A horse or mule can be attached to this marker, where there is a large field to be laid out. By marking the ground both ways, the labor of cultivation is much lessened; for the horse-cultivator can be run both ways, leaving very little to be done by hand.

*Transplanting.*—For Fall or Winter use, we begin planting in the field about the middle of June, and expect to finish by the first week in July.

Moist or damp weather is desirable for transplanting. The plants are first pulled from the seed-bed, and at once placed carefully in large baskets or boxes. The long tap-roots are shortened to about three inches. Each person is then furnished with a "dibble," which is made, by cutting off the upper end of a common digging-fork handle, leaving a shank about four inches long. This shank is made smooth and round, and slightly pointed on the lower end. Expert gardeners have a round iron shoe to slip over this shank, so that, while planting, the earth will not adhere to the dibble.

The baskets of plants are placed at regular distances across the field, so that a handful of plants taken from basket No. 1 will plant the row as far as basket No. 2, and so on. The operator holds the dibble in his right hand and a bundle of plants in the left; a hole is made at each intersection, and the root of a plant placed in it, when, by another movement of the dibble, the plant is fastened and the soil made level around the stem—only requiring three movements of the dibble to fasten a plant.

86 CABBAGES.

The rule among gardeners is, that the plant should be fastened so firmly, that, when the edge of one of the leaves is taken hold of by the thumb and

CABBAGE PLANT.

## CABBAGES.

finger, the piece of leaf would be torn off before the plant could be pulled out of place. In setting plants in dry weather, we sometimes dip the roots in a solution made of cow-manure and water, thick enough so that a portion of it adheres to the roots of the plants.

SCARIFIER.

On our farm a day's work for a man is six thousand five hundred plants, set in the way above directed. When hurried, we frequently transplant seven thousand plants in ten hours. So that, when there are three or four men planting at that rate, they will very soon put out one hundred thousand plants.

For a week or so from the time of planting, unless the weather is very moist, the plants will wilt some during the middle of the day. But just as soon as they fairly hold up their heads, a cultivator should be run between the rows, to disturb the surface and prevent the weeds from starting.

At first, running the cultivator one way will be enough. When the plants have made a good start and the leaves are larger, then the root-cleaner or Carrot-weeder can be run through the rows crosswise. This, when carefully done, will leave little or nothing to be done with the hand-hoe. The Carrot-weeder, Perry's scarifier, and Mapes' one-horse lifting sub-soil plough, are the only tools that we use in cultivating Cabbages. Heavy rains sometimes harden the surface; then the sub-soil is run once in each row, three or four inches deep, to break up the crust. The Carrot-weeder and scarifier (taking off the ploughs of the latter) are kept constantly going during the early part of the growing season—in fact, until the size of the leaves fills up the space between the rows.

ONE HORSE SUB-SOIL PLOUGH.

The object is not to run deep, but simply keep the surface loose and free from weeds. Unfavorable or wet weather often prevents the use of these horse-tools until the weeds have gained some headway. Over this no cultivator has any control; he can only make the best use of the means at hand, and adapt his work to circumstances; for every dollar saved in cultivating is a dollar earned. The *desideratum* being the production, on an acre, of the greatest number of large-sized heads of Cabbage at the least possible expense, at the same time keeping the soil in good heart.

If the plants are set two by two and a half feet apart, there will be eight thousand nine hundred on an acre. When there are no losses from diseases or insects, growers calculate that there will be six thousand five hundred to seven thousand marketable heads. At fifty dollars per thousand, this would give about three hundred and fifty dollars; then, deducting one hundred dollars for expenses, there will be left two hundred and fifty dollars profit on an acre. Taking one year with another, these figures will be found nearly correct. We have, the present season, received over six hundred dollars from an acre of Fall Cabbages; but prices averaged higher than usual.

Those who grow late Cabbages for market, always bury them in the field until such time as they are wanted—in mid-winter or towards Spring. We usually bury from twenty to fifty thousand heads every year, and seldom lose, by rotting, anything worth mentioning. We begin to bury Cabbages for Winter use from the 15th to the 25th of November, always, however, being guided by the weather. In case the weather is warm and pleasant along toward the middle of the month, then the work is put off until a later day; while, on the contrary, with cold, frosty nights, and no growth, the work of pulling the Cabbages and placing them in "beds" is pushed forward with all possible haste. White frost seldom does any injury to Winter Cabbages; but if the heads are left exposed to two or three successive nights of hard, black frost, the Cabbages will not keep well, and will probably rot badly before Spring. Therefore it is better, in the latitude of New York, to pull and bury the Cabbages on or before the 25th of November, to be sure that the outside leaves are not injured by frost.

At the time of pulling, each man is provided with a stick about three feet long and one and a quarter inches in diameter. This stick is carried in the right hand, to be used as a pry while pulling the Cabbage, and, when the head is turned upside down, for knocking the earth from the roots. Beginning at one side of the field, every man takes two rows of Cabbages, and, as he pulls, sorts them into two sizes. The large, solid heads are thrown into one line, while the second size, or small, hard heads, are put by themselves into another. This plan we find to work better than huddling the heads all together, large and small. It sometimes happens, in the Winter, that a customer wants a load all of one kind, either large or small; and when they are in separate beds, there is no trouble in getting out, at the time, just what is wanted.

When the Cabbages are all pulled, a suitable spot, or ridge, is chosen to make the bed; or a continuous line of beds across or the length of the patch. A narrow strip, eight feet wide, of ground that is a little higher than the adjoining surface, is preferable for the purpose. The Cabbages from either side, for a distance of ten or twelve feet, are carried to this chosen line, and one man places them close together, heads down and roots up. We make these beds

## CABBAGES.

eight feet wide, and of such length as to save time by not carrying the Cabbages unnecessary distances. Sometimes a bed is forty feet long; then a vacant space of the same length, then another bed of twenty-five or thirty feet, and so on from one end of the lot to the other. The principal object is to have the outside lines of the rows of beds straight, as it will make much easier work in putting on the covering of earth. The second-sized heads may be placed in the same row, but in separate beds. When Cabbages have done well, there will not be more than a fifth of the crop that will come under the second size; but it often happens that one-half, or a third, are small, and, of course, the beds of large and small will be alternate. Three active men will pull and place properly in beds twelve thousand Cabbages in a working-day of nine hours; and with a pair of horses and a plough the same number of men will cover twenty thousand in a day.

When pulled and placed in beds, heads down, they may be left without covering with earth for two or three weeks, suffering no injury, provided the weather is warm and mild. In fact, under such circumstances it is better to leave them uncovered until steady cold weather begins.

When the beds are all laid, then, with a plough and two horses, three furrows are turned towards the line of beds on either side. The first furrow-slice is turned close to the Cabbages, covering them, if possible. By means of shovels, the loose earth on each side is thrown over the Cabbages, covering all the heads and an inch or so of the stocks. When the bed is finished, there should be nothing visible except the roots and part of the stocks. The less quantity of soil that is used to do this, the better; for Cabbages will keep longer and in finer condition with two than with four inches of soil as a covering. The greater the depth of soil put on, beyond the amount necessary to cover the leaves, the more difficult it will be, in the Winter, to take them out as they are wanted.

Many Cabbage-growers still practise placing the Cabbages close together, in single rows, heads down, and then turning a furrow from either side toward the Cabbages. When the plough fails to cover all the heads, the work is finished with hand-hoes.

The curled leaved varieties of Savoy will do better if "heeled in," with the heads up, in the way described for keeping seed Cabbages. They will boil more tender when kept in this way than with the heads buried, although they will keep well when protected the same as other Winter varieties of Cabbage.

Those who are fond of Cabbage-greens, in the Spring, can have plenty of them by saving the stocks and heeling them in after the Cabbages have been cut off during the Fall. Early in the Spring these stocks are taken from their Winter quarters and planted out in some nook or corner of the garden. Very soon the young Cabbage-sprouts may be gathered in abundance, before Spring vegetables are ripe. German gardeners adopt this plan of saving the stocks and transplanting them into the field in the Spring, to raise the sprouts for market.

## CABBAGES.

INSECTS.—The most formidable insect with which the Cabbage-grower has to contend with is the *Anthomyia brassicæ*. It causes what is commonly known as "club-root." This disease is not confined to the Cabbage; the whole Brassica tribe suffers more or less from it.

On our place we cannot grow Cabbages two years in succession, on the same ground, without losing the whole crop by the "club-root;" and even every alternate year is not safe for late Cabbages.

The *Anthomyia brassicæ* is, in appearance, like the house-fly, only smaller. The eggs are deposited in the root of the Cabbage just below the surface. In ten or twelve days they hatch, and the small maggots begin at once to feed on the root, thus producing the well-known disease. The root becomes enlarged, and the leaves wilt badly under a hot sun, and the plant will not increase in size.

Last year I offered a premium of one hundred dollars for a remedy, and received a large number of communications in reply. Fourteen of them recommended the application of lime in almost as many different ways. Our soil is a heavy clay, the *débris* of red sandstone, and sprinkling lime broadcast did not check nor prevent the insects from injuring the plants. On a piece of ground where Cabbages had been grown the year before, we applied a dressing of lime at the rate of two hundred bushels to the acre, and again planted it with Cabbages. They were badly affected with club-root. One correspondent said that caustic shell-lime should be applied, using about a teaspoonful to each plant, by

5*

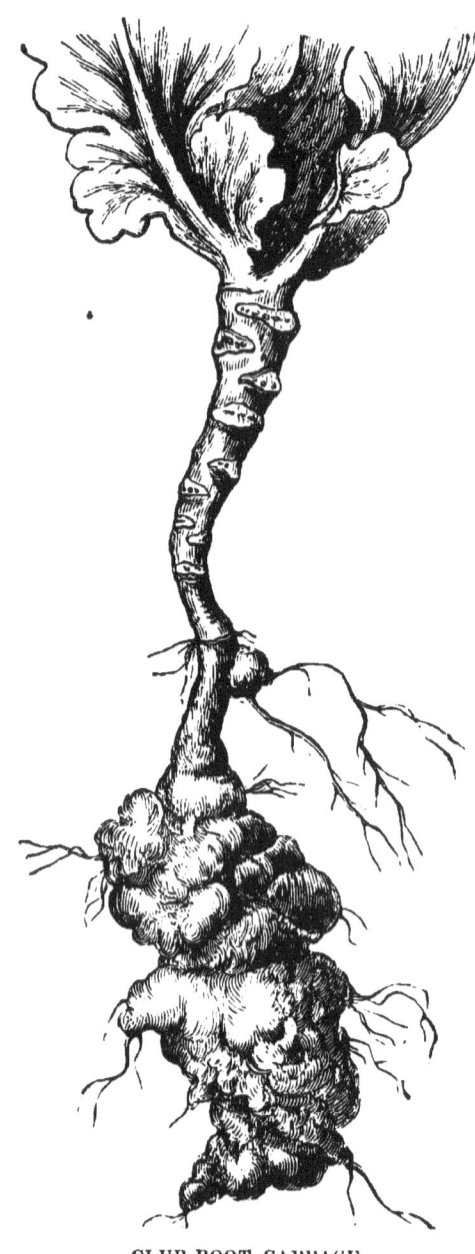

CLUB-ROOT CABBAGE.

removing a little earth from around the stem, putting on the lime, and then replacing the soil. This method, with dusting the roots of the Cabbage plants with fine bone-flour before setting them in place, has given me the best results. I will try them separately and in connection next year, and will then be a better judge as to which to give the credit.

There is no doubt in my mind but that lime does check the insect; for I have known many instances where Cabbages have been grown ten or twelve years in succession on lime-soils, and not a case of clubroot has occurred.

*Pieris rapæ.*—Cabbage Worm. This insect, introduced from Europe into Canada in 1857, made its first appearance in New Jersey, and others of the Middle States, as well as in some of the Southern States, last year. But already its ravages on the Cabbage and Turnip crops have caused serious alarm among those who cultivate these vegetables to any extent.

The worm is of a light-green color, large body, and, when full-grown, three-fourths of an inch in length. It eats the Cabbage-leaves with an astounding rapidity. Mr. Sprague, of Boston, has described, in the *American Entomologist*, Vol. II., page 370, a small beetle, which is probably parasitic on the *Anthomyia brassicæ.*

These worms made their first appearance on our Cabbage-field about the 27th of July. They appeared so suddenly and in such numbers as to render it impossible to remove them by hand. One woman in our neighborhood attempted it with her patch; she picked off two pailsful, in three days, from three hundred heads of Cabbage; and while she was doing so, the green parts of the Cabbages were nearly all demolished. Where there were fifty thousand Cabbages in a piece, this way of removal was not practicable.

We immediately set to work and sprinkled the Cabbages with lime, hoping this would drive them off; but it had not the slightest effect in arresting their depredations. At this time a friend broke off a Cabbage-leaf with one of these worms upon it, and dusted the surface of the leaf and the body of the worm with lime, so that he might closely watch the result. While in this condition it ate a square inch of the leaf in forty-two minutes. This was a satisfactory evidence that the lime would not stop nor at all inconvenience the worms while destroying the Cabbage-leaves.

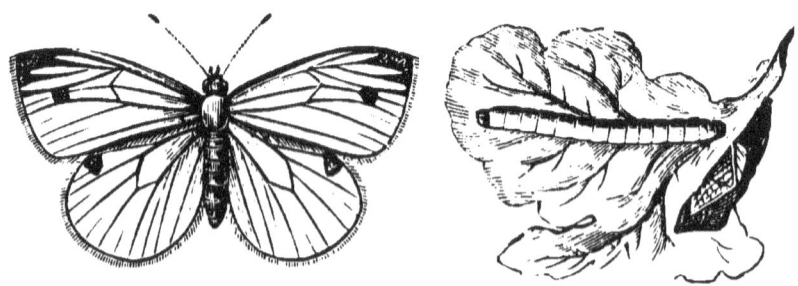

WORM AND MOTH (*Pieris rapæ*).

We then applied fine salt, carbolic powder, and a dozen other specifics, but without any success. At last we mixed with twenty parts of superphosphate of lime, one part of carbolic powder, and three parts of fresh air-slacked lime. These were thoroughly mixed, and a small quantity of the compound thrown by hand into each head of Cabbage. This was repeated three times, with the most satisfactory results. In some localities it may be found necessary to apply the remedy oftener. Our crop was not injured five per cent. The heads damaged most were in sheltered places near the fences. Many of these moths may be caught with a net, by boys, where they do not appear in too large numbers.

There were three distinct broods of these worms, hatched and fed on the Cabbages, from the time they appeared in July until cold weather. The last lot was not so destructive as the first or second. In some localities the early Cabbages are attacked and injured badly by a small maggot, similar in appearance to the Onion-maggot (*Anthomyia ceparum*). Caustic lime, or fine flour of bone, applied in the way recommended for " club-root," is the best remedy that we have tried to check this pest.

### CARROT.

*Daucus carota.*

Many intelligent agricultural writers have for years persistently advocated the more general cultivation of the Carrot, not only for table use, but also on account of its high value for feeding-purposes. These views have been very slowly adopted by farmers, not because they in any way doubted the statements of these writers, or had any misgivings about the value of the Carrot for feeding stock, but they believed the cultivation of it was too expensive, often costing more than the worth of the crop. I know many instances where attempts have been made by good farmers to grow Carrots, but just at the time when the young plants were fairly above ground and needed immediate attention, the farmer was in the midst of harvesting his hay and grain. These had to be got through with, and the Carrots were left untouched for two or three weeks. By this time the weeds had gained such headway, that to attempt to clean the piece appeared like an endless job. The result was, that Carrots, weeds, and grass were ploughed under after all the trouble and expense of preparing the ground, cost of seed, sowing it, &c. With Potatoes, Cabbages, or Corn, a week or ten days will make but little difference in the time of the first hoeing, provided the ground is in good heart. But with Carrots this loss of time is irreparable, for, unless the ground between the rows is disturbed just when the Carrots are coming up, the weeds will get ahead, and it will require a season's labor to make up the loss sustained by a few days' neglect at the commencement. It should be distinctly borne in mind by those who intend to grow Carrots for profit, that "a stitch in time saves nine," and that early and frequent disturbance of the ground materially lessens the expense of cultivating Carrots.

SOIL.—The Carrot will do well on any character of soil that is deep, free from stones, and well manured. A sandy loam is frequently recommended for it; but, from my experience, I am in favor of a heavier soil, that has been thoroughly pulverized and made fine by two or three ploughings before sowing the seed. Our method is, to Fall-plough, and then give two ploughings and harrowings in the Spring. This will leave the ground in fine tilth. The manure is spread broadcast on the surface before the last ploughing, and covered. Before harrowing the last time, the surface should be top-dressed with some special manure or compost, to insure a vigorous start for the young Carrots.

On heavy soil, it is best to make drills, or ridges, instead of sowing the seed on the flat. This plan enables one to pass a Carrot horse-weeder between the rows early, without injuring the young and delicate plants as they are coming through the surface. These ridges are made with one horse and a small plough, commencing on one side of the field and throwing two furrows together, forming ridges, the tops of which should be five or six inches above the level of the surface, and from twenty-four to twenty-seven inches apart. This space is wide enough to admit a horse or mule in cultivating.

HOLBROOK'S REGULATOR SEED-DRILL.

Sowing the Seed.—The tops of these ridges are then made fine by drawing a wooden rake or prong-hoe over each one, in the line of the ridges, carefully removing any hard lumps of clay, stones, &c., to the furrows between. The seed is sown by a machine, using four to five pounds of fresh seed to an acre. Carrot-seed can only be relied upon with certainty for one year. With seed two years old, I would increase the quantity to five or six pounds to the acre. It is an excellent plan to sow sparsely some white Spanish Radish-seed, or, in fact, any kind of Radish, in the drills at the time of sowing the Carrots. The Radishes will germinate much sooner than the Carrots, showing distinctly, in ten or twelve days, the lines of the rows, and thus enable the grower to cultivate much earlier than he otherwise could. When the Carrot-tops are three or four inches high, the Radishes may be pulled out, having fulfilled their mission. Market-gardeners turn these Radishes to account by preparing them for market.

For a Fall crop, the seed should be sown from the 20th of May to the 1st of June. A few days earlier or later than these dates will not make much difference, although it is better, in my estimation, to have the seed in the ground on or before the 1st of June. Holbrook's seed-drill is simple in construction—the best that I have tested for sowing garden-seeds.

CULTIVATING.—This, above all, is the most important point in growing Carrots profitably in the field. The moment that the Radishes are fairly above ground, and before the weeds have started, the spaces between the rows should be disturbed by a tool drawn by a horse or mule. This should be repeated within a week, and often enough afterward to keep down effectually the grass and weeds.

For many years I have used for this purpose two implements which I consider more simple and more effective than any others that have come under my notice—the Carrot-weeder, which does the work with light draft, and very thoroughly; and Mapes' one-horse lifting sub-soil plough. In case the ground between the rows becomes hard from heavy rains, a mule is attached to the "lifter," which is run once in each space between the rows, and three or four inches deep, lifting and loosening the soil without disturbing the roots. These are the only tools I use in the culture of Carrots, and I have no hesitation in stating that they are the best I have seen, simple in construction, and easily managed. With a few days' practice and a steady animal, a man or boy will run the Carrot-weeder as close to the rows of Carrots, without injury, as the common hand-hoe, and, of course, doing it thirty times as fast.

When this plan is carried out, the only hand-labor necessary is to remove what weeds may come up directly in the rows, and thin the Carrots at a later date.

About four weeks from the time of sowing the seed, the weeds and some of the Radishes should be pulled out by hand. The season, and other circumstances, will often vary this; it is not, however, wise to put off too long the first hand-weeding. Two or three weeks later, by the middle of July, the Carrots should be carefully thinned by hand, leaving them about four inches apart in the rows, at the same time removing any weeds that may have made their appearance since the last weeding. With an ordinary season, and the horse-tools kept actively going during the early part of it, the total expense for hand-labor, in weeding and thinning an acre of Carrots, will not exceed twenty-five dollars. The total cost of producing an acre of Carrots should not exceed sixty-five dollars.

An acre, under good cultivation, will yield from five to seven hundred bushels of Carrots, worth usually fifty cents per bushel. For the last five years I have sold all our crop for horse-feed at seventy-five cents per bushel, and never have any difficulty in finding purchasers, at this price by the quantity. The Carrot will, without doubt, become more popular from year to year with those who keep horses the greater part of the year on grain, especially for hard-worked draft-horses. This I know to be the case, from my experience in raising Carrots for market. Livery-stable keepers and express companies, who, ten or twelve years ago, would only order fifteen or twenty bushels of Carrots at a time, now buy them by the one hundred bushels during the Winter.

Harvesting Carrots.—In the latitude of New York, Carrots wanted for Winter use should be dug and pitted early in November. Two men will accomplish more work in gathering, topping, and storing Turnips, Carrots, or Beets, while the weather is mild, than four will do when cold weather has set in. Topping Turnips or Carrots in an open field, on a frosty morning, is anything but pleasant; and it is as expensive to the owner as it is disagreeable to the operator. On some farms it is customary to cart all the roots, as soon as pulled, into the barn. This adds expense and considerable extra labor to the harvesting of the crop—loading in the field and unloading at the barn. The time this requires may all be set down as unnecessary expense. Every hundred bushels of roots pulled and topped in the field, while the weather is pleasant and warm enough to make working out of doors comfortable, is a saving in expense of at least fifty per cent. This we have tested over and over again, and always with the same result.

Those who have grown Carrots as a field-crop, know how tedious a job it is to dig them in the Fall. It is not only tedious, but if the Carrots have grown full-size, unless taken out by careful workmen, there will be half a dozen fork or spade-handles broken in getting out an acre or two of Carrots.

We grow on our farm from eight hundred to one thousand bushels of Carrots every year for market, and we have many years since given up the use of the spade and digging-fork in taking out the crop. We do it with much less manual labor and less expense, by applying horse-power instead of man-power. The rows of Carrots are about two feet apart—wide enough for a horse or a mule to walk between. When the proper time arrives, and other things being in readiness, two horses are hitched to a lifting sub-soil plough, which is run alongside of each row of Carrots, deep enough to lift and loosen both earth and Carrots along the line of the row. This operation leaves every root so that it can be pulled readily by hand, having to use no more strength than would be required in pulling Strapleaved Red-top Turnips.

Plough on one side of the piece, running the "lifter" alongside of the right-hand row of Carrots, and returning on the left. This will bring the two cuts of the sub-soil between two rows, leaving the outside of these rows for the horses to walk on and have firm footing. With a pair of steady workhorses, a sub-soil plough, three men, and a boy to drive the horses, we have frequently loosened and pulled an acre of Carrots in a day. Occasionally, if the ground is stony, the plough will miss loosening a Carrot; but this will not cause a detention of any account to those pulling the roots. When pulled, the Carrots are thrown into small heaps; or, better still, three or four rows are thrown into a continuous row, with the roots all in one direction. This arrangement will facilitate the topping, which is the slowest part of the work of gathering the crop.

By the use of this plough, we have taken out and topped an acre of Carrots, that yielded five hundred bushels, at a total cost of nine dollars and fifty cents, or rather less than two cents a bushel. To dig and top the same number of bushels in the old-fashioned way, would cost, at the lowest estimate, three times as much. Six cents a bushel is usually estimated as the cost of digging and topping a bushel of Carrots. I mention all the particulars in this

## CARROTS.

case, to show the advantages of a more general use of improved labor-saving implements, in "trucking" as well as in more extended farming. Until such tools are more generally used, the lowest cost of producing a bushel of Potatoes or Carrots cannot be known. The sub-soil plough, used in getting out these Carrots, we have had on the farm ten years, and have used it more or less every year since. The first cost of the plough was thirteen dollars, and in a half-day's work loosening Carrots, the amount saved was more than had been paid for the plough ten years ago.

WINTERING.—Like most other kinds of roots, Carrots will keep very well when put into pits out of doors. If one has abundance of cellar-room, it is better to store them there until wanted; but when cellar-room is scarce, then, with care and a little more expense, they can be kept safely out of doors until April. In choosing a situation for a pit, a sloping surface is always preferable—a spot where there is a good natural fall for water. The surface of such a sloping piece of ground is simply levelled off six or seven feet wide, and as long as is required. The Carrots are then made into a long pile six feet wide, sloping gradually on either side, and coming to a point about three and a half to four feet high. Five or six hundred bushels may be piled together in this way, if, when putting on the covering of soil, means of ventilation are provided at points ten or fifteen feet apart along the top of the pile. This is done by placing a piece of tin or earthen pipe, with one end resting on the Carrots, the other projecting a couple of inches above the covering of earth. To prevent the frost from injuring the roots through the pipes, they may be stuffed with hay before Winter sets in. Formerly, the practice among gardeners was to put a covering of hay or straw over the roots before putting on the earth. This, of late years, has been given up as useless; in fact, it is found, by experience, that all kinds of roots will keep better, with less risk of rotting, when earth is the only covering used. Under ordinary circumstances, two feet in thickness of covering is quite enough to protect the roots from frost. It is not a good plan to put on this depth at once; eight inches will be sufficient when first pitted, and until the weather grows colder. All kinds of roots should be covered as soon as possible after being topped. If left exposed a day or two, either in small heaps in the field, or in a large pile, the shrinking from evaporation amounts to considerable—enough, at least, to call the attention of growers to the fact.

It is well, perhaps, to state, in this connection, that those who grow Carrots as a field or garden-crop should not neglect to save, at the time of gathering the crop, some of the best-formed and largest-sized roots for seed. Fresh Carrot-seed, *true to name*, is all-important for those who grow Carrots either for pleasure or profit.

In topping seed Carrots, it is not well to cut as close to the crown of the Carrot as is customary with the main crop.

# CARROTS.

The directions given for keeping Carrots out of doors are equally applicable to Beets, Turnips, and Parsnips.

With the last-mentioned, when intended for market, the pile should be made smaller — not more than five feet wide and three feet high. Parsnips, put together for Winter use in larger heaps, change color, becoming a straw-yellow. This will injure the sale sometimes, making a difference of from fifty cents to one dollar a barrel. In fact, yellow Parsnips find no purchasers as long as there are any white ones in market.

In garden-culture, Carrots may be planted closer together, fifteen to eighteen inches between the rows, and thinned out to three or four inches apart in the row. If wanted for Summer use, they must be sown early in April. Two ounces of seed will be enough to sow for family use.

VARIETIES.— There are but few varieties worthy of cultivation, either for home consumption or market use.

EARLY HORN is a variety sometimes grown by market-gardeners, to sell by the bunch in July. The root never attains much size, and is therefore only used for this purpose.

LONG ORANGE is the best variety for the main crop, both for field and garden-culture. When planted on good soil, it has a long, smooth root, Orange color, and of good quality. The roots will average twelve to fifteen inches in length.

BLISS' IMPROVED LONG ORANGE resembles the above. The only difference is, that the color is darker and the roots are somewhat smoother and longer than the Long Orange.

WHITE BELGIUM grows out of the ground like a long Beet. It is nearly white, and yields more to the acre than any other kind of Carrot we have grown; but it does not sell readily in market.

## CARDOON.

*Cynara cardunculus.*

This vegetable, in appearance, resembles the Globe Artichoke, but, with good treatment, it will grow taller than the Artichoke. It is seldom found in the kitchen-gardens of this country, although, when carefully grown and blanched, the stocks make pleasant salads. They are also used in soups and stews; but, for either purpose, the Cardoon is very much inferior to Celery.

LONG ORANGE.

The seeds should be sown in May, in drills an inch deep and three feet apart. When the plants are well above ground, they should be thinned out to twenty inches apart in the row, and the soil kept loose and free from weeds. In October, the leaves should be drawn together and fastened by hay-bands, and the plants earthed up the same as Celery. The Cardoon can be kept in the same way as Celery through the Winter. One ounce of seed will give five to six hundred plants.

CAULIFLOWER.

*Brassica oleracea botrytis.*

The Cauliflower is so closely allied to the Broccoli, that the culture recommended for the one will answer in every respect for the other. We usually grow the Cauliflower as a Spring crop, and the Broccoli for a Fall crop. When the Cauliflower succeeds, it is one of the most profitable crops grown by the market-gardener; and the private gardener, who is successful with it, gives unusual satisfaction to his employer. Cauliflowers rarely sell for less than fifteen dollars per hundred, and, very often, well-formed heads sell freely at eighteen or twenty dollars per hundred by the quantity.

Our method is, to sow the seed about the 10th of September (one ounce will give three thousand five hundred plants), and in four or five weeks prick the plants into cold frames, five or six hundred to a sash. These frames are covered with sashes during the Winter, which are opened on mild days to give air, and removed as the weather grows warm towards Spring. The seed may also be sown, in February, in a hot-bed, and transplanted once or twice before the final planting in the field. We have always succeeded better with cold-frame plants for Cauliflower.

There is no use in attempting to grow Cauliflower, with any hope of success, either in the garden or field, on a poorly-worked or poorly-manured ground. There should be plenty of well-rotted horse-manure ploughed under, at least eighty two-horse loads to the acre, and then a slight top-dressing, two or three hundred pounds of Peruvian guano or finely-ground bone spread broadcast before planting, or at the first hoeing around the plants.

When the plants are wintered in a cold frame, they may be set in the open ground early in April, and the heads will be well formed before the hot weather in July. With late Spring planting it is almost impossible to get Cauliflowers to form any heads. The flowers will "button," and, in eight cases out of ten, the crop will not cover expenses. Two years ago we planted twelve hundred in a piece of rich ground on the 15th of May; they were a total failure, not producing ten good heads.

For a Fall crop, the seed may be sown at the same time as for Winter Cabbage, and planted in the field at the same distance apart, about the middle of July.

The early kinds may be set closer together, two feet apart each way. When a crop succeeds, it will bring from seven hundred to one thousand dollars on an acre.

The number of varieties cultivated is quite limited. If the private gardener will select, for planting in the kitchen-garden, such kinds as are popular with market-gardeners, he will be sure to make no mistake

EARLY PARIS is one of the reliable varieties, and a favorite with cultivators. Under good treatment, it forms solid heads, that are, when cooked, tender and delicate in quality. When grown on a rich soil, the leaves spread more than some of the other kinds.

EARLY ERFURT is an earlier variety, ripening a few days in advance of the Early Paris. It does not require so much room, as it is of dwarfish habits, but it forms a solid white head of first-rate quality.

HALF-EARLY PARIS is a popular kind, maturing later than either of the above. We have grown it as a late variety, with good success, both in the garden and field.

WALCHEREN is better suited for late than for early planting. The heads are generally uniform in size and compactness, and of very good quality.

The same kinds of insects that injure Cabbage also damage Cauliflower. Last season this crop suffered more from the ravages of the *Pieris rapae* than the late Cabbages. I have seen thousands of half-grown Cauliflowers rendered worthless from *club-root*. The cut-worm *Agrotis devastator* destroys the Cauliflower as well as Cabbage-plants. The best remedy is, to search for them and kill them with the thumb and finger. We saved twenty thousand Cabbages one season by this method.

When Cauliflowers are planted in the open field in April, the crop will mature in time to plant Celery in July or Spinach in September.

### CELERY.

*Apium graveolens.*

Market-gardeners in the vicinity of New York always plant Celery as a second crop, following Early

Cabbages, Onions, Beets, or Potatoes. The ground is heavily manured in the Spring for these crops, and, as soon as they are removed and marketed in July, it is ploughed and put in order for Celery. The surface is made fine and mellow by the harrow. In case the soil turns up rough, owing to heavy rains or continued dry weather, a light roller run over the surface will facilitate the work and lessen the expense of crushing the lumps, leaving the ground level and smooth, ready for planting. In the small kitchen-garden, the same conditions of depth and tilth must be brought about by the use of the digging-fork, spade, and hand-rake. If the ground intended for Celery was not liberally manured in the Spring, and doubts are entertained as to the fertility of the soil, it is well to add a heavy dressing of well-rotted barn-yard manure, spread broadcast, and plough or fork it under before planting. It is a waste of time and money to attempt to grow Celery on poor soil.

The old-fashioned system of making deep trenches with the spade, in which to plant Celery, practised so extensively twelve or fifteen years ago, has been abandoned, of late, by the progressive market-gardener as a useless expense, without a single redeeming feature. It has been found, by experience, that Celery will do very much better planted on the surface of the same quality of soil, making much quicker and larger growth, and thus saving all that unnecessary labor and expense of digging trenches. This was an important move in the right direction, increasing the products of the soil by a system which tasks the brain of the gardener as well as his muscle; or, in other words, we see physical strength, in a properly-managed market-garden, becoming subservient to systematic and maturely developed plans.

The time of planting Celery varies according to the disposition to be made of the crop, from the 20th of June to the 15th of August. Planted in rich ground before the 20th of July, it will, under favorable circumstances, be large enough to be banked, bleached, and sold by the latter part of October and through the month of November.

Celery will succeed best when planted in a deep, rich loam, which has been well pulverized previously.

SOWING THE SEED.—The seed of Celery should be sown in the open ground, in a sheltered border, as early in April as the soil is dry enough to be worked. Before sowing, the seed-bed should have a heavy dressing of well-rotted barn-yard manure, scattered evenly over the surface and forked under; then raked, removing any hard lumps of soil, stones, &c., &c., leaving the ground loose and finely pulverized. Open shallow drills with the marker one foot apart; sow the seed thinly in the drills by hand, and cover the seed by raking the surface with a wooden rake, drawing it in the line of the drills. We sow some Radish seed sparsely in the drills at the time of sowing the Celery-seed. The Radish will germinate in a few days, showing the line of the rows, when a scuffle-hoe can be used between them, before the weeds start to grow. If the weeds get ahead, the labor will be increased tenfold. When the plants are three or four inches high, cut off the tops; this can be repeated a second time to advantage. It will encourage a stocky growth of plants, that will be more uniform in size. Market-gardeners who grow Celery in a large way should, every Fall, at the time of digging, select some of the best specimen stalks from which to raise seed. By following this plan, the size and quality are improved each year, and there is no disappointment about poor seed not coming up.

On sandy soil it is often advisable to run a light roller over the seed-bed soon after the seed is sown.

PLANTING.—When everything is in readiness for planting, the garden-line is sketched on one side of the piece, and then, with the "marker"—the teeth set at three feet apart for the dwarf kinds, or four for the larger growing sorts—the lines are marked out straight. There is nothing that gives a more careless appearance to a vegetable-garden than crooked rows of Celery.

It is well, just before planting, to sprinkle along the lines of the intended rows some wood-ashes, fine bone-dust, or superphosphate; either of which should be mixed with twice its own bulk of soil before application. When applied in this way, the young plants get a good start early in the season—a point of the highest importance in growing Celery for market.

It is better, under all circumstances, to select damp or wet weather for transplanting. In pulling the plants from the seed-bed, get them of uniform size, so that the growth in the garden or field, under good treatment, may be about the same. Both roots and leaves of Celery plants should be trimmed before setting out; that is, the plants are taken in handfuls, and, with a sharp case-knife, a portion of the roots is cut off, leaving about two inches and a half, and all the outside leaves are cut off even with the top of the heart. They are then set firmly in rows, with the dibble, from five to six inches apart, and never any deeper than they were in the seed-bed. The earth on either side of the plants should be pressed with the feet; this will, in a measure, prevent its drying out. If the weather should set in very dry and hot immediately after planting, nail two boards together, the end-view of which would resemble the letter Λ, and place this structure over the plants in the row. It will keep the ground moist enough to start them growing in a few days.

There will be no occasion for this covering if the ground is moist at the time of planting, or the weather keeps cloudy for a short time. This precaution is only put in practice in case of continued dry weather, which always more or less injures Celery when recently transplanted.

During the early stages of growth, the only thing to be done is to keep the spaces between the rows disturbed frequently. In field-culture this can be done at a much less expense by horse than by manpower. In garden-culture, the hand-hoe and rake are the only tools required for a month or six weeks after planting. When the Celery is twelve or fifteen inches long, the earth on either side of the row should be loosened two or three inches deep with a cultivator, sub-soil plough, or hand-hoe. It is then ready for "handling," which should be done with care.

This operation is simple, but requires some practice before much headway can be made. The operator gets down on his knees, gathers all the leaves of each stalk up, and, while holding them in position with one hand, presses the loosened earth against the stalk with the other; then *vice-versâ*, going in this way the length of the row, and each row in turn. When this is finished, the earth is thrown toward the Celery from both sides with a one-horse plough. A man usually follows with a hand-hoe and draws the earth still closer to the Celery, where the plough missed or failed to do the work well. In the garden, the hoe is made use of instead of the plough. As fast as the Celery grows, the earth is drawn up by men with hoes, until the time for banking, in order to make the hearts white; or "bleaching," as it is usually termed by gardeners.

This part of the work is more tedious, and, to do it well, calls for a person who knows how to handle the spade. A man stands on either side of the same row, and, commencing about ten or twelve inches from the Celery, raises a straight bank of earth, covering all the Celery except three or four inches of the ends of the longest leaves. Each man endeavors to build his side firmly, and straight up and down. It is usually a matter of considerable pride among practical gardeners, their ability to bank Celery well.

This walling up the Celery begins about the middle of September, and, when it is grown on a large scale, as it is in the vicinity of New York, this banking continues until cold weather—especially for all that is intended for sale during the Fall or early Winter. The portion reserved for sale after the holidays is not generally banked in the way described, but is put into Winter quarters, where the same results are brought about. The only difference is in the length of time required. In this respect the Fall banking has the advantage. In drawing earth toward the Celery, and in banking with the spade, it is very important that the hearts should be kept straight, not broken, nor in any way injured by carelessness.

To KEEP CELERY IN WINTER.—Formerly there was a very large percentage of loss in trying to keep Celery during the Winter. The hearts are very tender, and rot easily when buried in the old-fashioned style. Of late, gardeners in this neighborhood have hit upon a much better and more simple method, of which the private gardener or farmer may avail himself as readily as the professional market-gardener.

In the Middle States, Celery is usually taken up from the 1st to the 20th of November. To facilitate the removal of the earth from the rows, we make use of a large-sized single plough, and then, by following with a lifting sub-soil, the stalks are all loosened without the aid of the spade. The stalks are then pulled up, some of the earth shaken from the roots, and left in heaps along the row. In the meantime a trench is opened in some convenient spot, ten inches wide, the depth to correspond with the length of the Celery. Some loose earth is left on the bottom of the trench, which it is always better to make where there is a natural fall for the water to run off, especially on clay ground. The Celery is carried to the edge of the trench, and, beginning at the upper or higher end, is placed in an upright position, closely packed together, until the whole trench is filled. As the weather grows colder the earth is drawn from either side toward the Celery, and when the covering is entirely finished, it looks like a single row of Celery banked up.

The Celery-tops should be dry when packed away in trenches, otherwise it may rot badly. The bleaching process will be hastened by pressing some fine earth in along side of the stalks at the time of stowing the crop away. The tops are preserved by covering them with long manure, salt hay, or any other litter, provided it is put on in sufficient quantity.

The boards recommended as a protection for the young plants from the sun can be made use of for this purpose; they will be found serviceable. The front of such a pit or trench can at all times be opened with but little trouble, even in very cold or inclement weather.

This is by far the best method for keeping Celery during the Winter with which I am familiar, and market-gardeners near New York have very generally adopted it. In case the bleaching goes on too slowly in cold weather, it may be quickened by removing the top covering and pouring a stream of tepid water into the trench, to moisten the roots. The hay, manure, or boards, should then be immediately replaced, to prevent the frost from injuring the leaves of the Celery.

To Prepare Celery for Market.—It is a fact well known to market-gardeners, that each kind of vegetable, in order to command the highest price, must be prepared in a certain way; and if this arbitrary rule is not strictly adhered to, the produce will not bring half of what it otherwise would. There appears to be no obvious reason why nine long Radishes tied in a round bunch are not as good as the same nine tied in a flat one; nor why three or four stalks of Celery made up into a round bunch are not as palatable and in every way as good as when made into a flat bunch. Still, in the one case, they will find plenty of customers at the best market rates; while, in the other, there is no demand, and they would not bring enough to pay expenses.

The methods in general use for preparing certain kinds of vegetables for market, are expensive and laborious to the producer. Talking on this subject, a few days ago, with a market-gardener, he remarked that it was more trouble to prepare and market some kinds of "truck" than it was to grow them, and he named Celery as an example. The bulk of this crop is sold during the Winter months, and nearly all the time from the middle of December to the middle of March is spent in preparing it for market. The stalks are first taken from the trench to the market-house. This building is provided with a stove, boilers for heating water, a large wash-tub, and two tables, arranged one on each side of the tub. The stalks are then trimmed by taking off some of the outside leaves, so as to expose the heart; the root is shaved with a long-bladed knife, leaving four flat sides, tapering a little toward the end; and the operator cuts a narrow circular groove in about the same position on each root, to facilitate tying.

The stalks, having been sorted at the time of trimming, are now placed in the wash-tub, and, with plenty of warm water and a scrubbing-brush, the Celery is thoroughly cleansed and put out on the tables for bunching. This last operation requires the most skill and practice. A gardener who is expert at bunching Celery can always command higher wages on that account.

The bass matting, or twine, is cut the proper lengths and fastened in a convenient place near the person bunching, who stands in front of the table. Three or four stalks are selected for each bunch, according to the size of the Celery. These stalks are arranged to the best advantage, and the roots are tied closely together by making a single knot around each one, except the last, which has a double or fastening-knot; care being taken to have the outside stalks trimmed nearly alike, so as to make the bunch symmetrical. The tops and all the small stocks are made into round bunches, and sold at a low price for soup Celery.

A person who is expert in bunching will tie four or five dozen an hour, day after day, for weeks at a time, working day and night, I might say; for the market-gardener seldom gets through his work in "Celery-time" before 9 or 10 o'clock at night. The morning is usually devoted to getting in the Celery from the trenches, and the afternoon and evening to trimming and bunching.

When the day's work is finished, the bunches are counted and carefully placed in chests made expressly for the purpose, and forwarded to market.

Profits.—Under the former laborious and crude method of cultivating Celery, there was but little profit attached to the crop. It cost, then, from one to one and a half cents a root to grow it; this, with the large percentage of loss from rotting during the Winter, left but a small margin for profit. The plan now in general use among gardeners in New Jersey reduces the expense to a half or three-quarters of a cent a root; and in connection with this, by the improved method for keeping it through the Winter, the profits are decidedly increased. When Celery is planted at the distances named, there can be grown on an acre about twenty-six thousand roots. It rarely happens that more than twenty thousand of these are of full size, and worth two and a half cents a root, which would give five hundred dollars for the acre. The balance of the small stocks, tied in round bunches and sold at low prices, would add twenty or thirty dollars to the above amount.

This looks like a large sum—and it would be, if there were no losses nor heavy expenses in producing the crop; but it must be marked down as one of the most expensive and troublesome with which the market-gardener has to deal.

Varieties.—Among the many changes that have been introduced in the culture of Celery for market, there is none more apparent than the sudden somer-

## CELERY.

sault made by gardeners in giving up the cultivation of the tall growing kinds for the dwarf varieties. The latter have rapidly increased in favor, not only

WHITE SOLID.

with growers, but also with consumers. The reasons for making this change are clearly practical, and no wide-awake gardener will overlook them. The dwarf sorts can be planted more closely together, giving several thousands more roots to the acre than the taller kinds; besides, there is a larger proportion of "heart" to every stock, and the quality is equally good.

There are not many varieties of Celery worthy of cultivation, either for market or for family use Of the best, may be named:

WHITE SOLID.—This has long been held as a favorite tall-growing kind. The hearts, when bleached, are white and crisp, and very delicate in flavor.

SEYMOUR'S SUPERB grows larger than the WHITE SOLID. It is esteemed among gardeners as the most profitable, for market, of any of the tall varieties. The hearts are large, round, and solid.

INCOMPARABLE DWARF.—This is in all respects the best dwarf variety for field or garden-culture. The stalks grow on an average from twenty inches to two feet in length.

When bleached, the hearts are of a dull white, crisp, very solid, and of excellent quality.

BOSTON MARKET is more extensively grown around Boston than in the vicinity of New York. It is a dwarf variety, producing a large proportion of "heart" to every stock, of very superior quality, and of mild flavor. It is not, in my estimation, in any way superior, as a market variety, to the Incomparable Dwarf.

There are several sorts of Red Celery, but there is so little demand for them in market, it hardly pays to trouble one's self with them. In the kitchen-

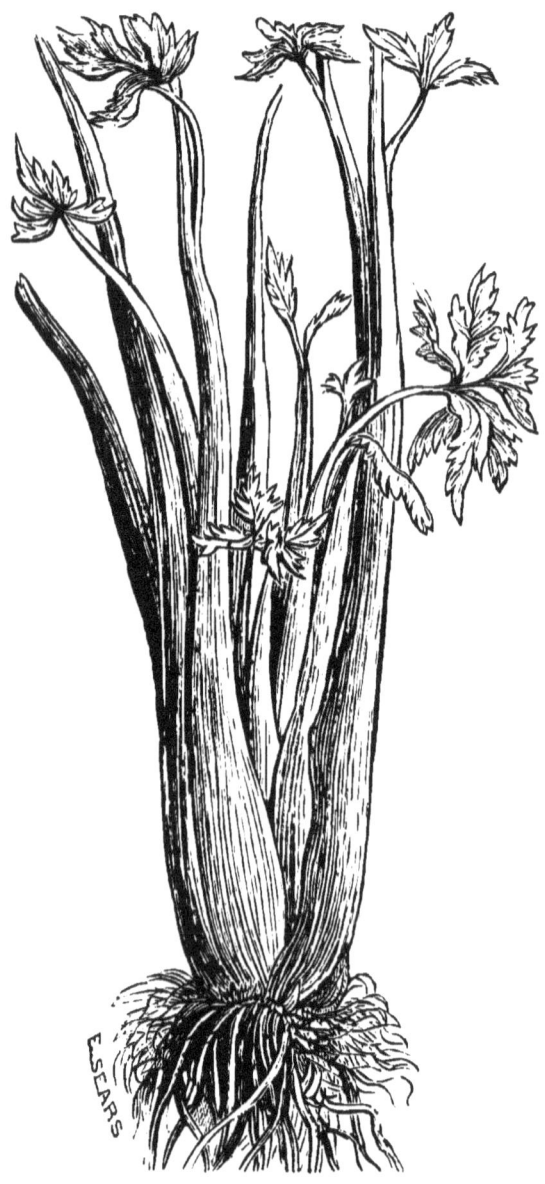

INCOMPARABLE DWARF.

garden, where a variety may be wanted, plant a few of the

DWARF CRIMSON.—In habits of growth it is very similar to the other dwarf kinds, only differing in color. The hearts are crisp, solid, and of a dark crimson color.

For family use, one thousand plants will keep the table well supplied during the Fall and Winter. No garden should be considered complete without a supply of Celery. One ounce of fresh seed will give five to six thousand plants. A couple of small packages of seed, costing twelve cents, will furnish plants enough—if they are taken care of—to stock the kitchen-garden.

Growing the plants for sale is a large branch of business in some sections. They are usually worth from three to five dollars per thousand in lots of from five to ten thousand.

CELERIAC.—Celeriac, or Turnip-rooted Celery, is now cultivated to a considerable extent by some market-gardeners. It is used principally by Germans, who boil and slice the root and then make it into a Salad.

The seed should be sown at the same time and be treated in the same manner as Celery-seed. When transplanted into the open ground, the rows may be marked two feet apart, and the plants set six inches apart in the row. It requires no earthing-up, and on this account, if there was sufficient demand for it, Celeriac would be more profitable to grow than Celery, as it usually brings the same price in market.

It is stored for Winter in trenches, the same as Celery.

CELERIAC.

## CORN SALAD, OR FETTICUS.

*Valeriana locusta.*

The Corn Salad, familiarly known in some sections under the name of Fetticus, or Lamb's Quarter, is used for a Salad in early Spring, and is cultivated in every respect like Spinach.

The seed should be sown early in September, in drills, one foot apart and half an inch deep. The spaces between the rows should be hoed once during the Fall, and, as far north as New York, mulched with salt hay or straw during the Winter. In the Spring the mulch is taken off, and the Corn Salad will be ready for use in April and May. The seed may be sown in the Spring, but when grown in hot weather the quality is inferior. Two ounces of seed will be enough for family use, and for an acre it will require six pounds.

The plants left uncut will run up to seed in the Summer, and any one desirous can easily obtain pure seed in this way.

## CRESS, OR PEPPERGRASS.

*Lepidium sativum.*

Cress, or Peppergrass, is a hardy annual, used as a Salad in this country. Owing to its well-known tendency to run to seed, two or three successive sowings should be made, two weeks apart. The first seed may be sown as early in April as the ground can be worked.

Make drills one foot apart, and cover lightly.

One ounce of seed will be sufficient for three separate sowings. The last one should be made in some shaded spot in the garden; as it will do better, sheltered from the direct rays of the sun in Summer.

The leaves should be cut for a Salad when young, before they become rough.

There are many varieties, but the CURLED CRESS will be found best for cultivation.

## WATER-CRESS.

*Sisymbrium nasturtium.*

Water-Cress is a very common aquatic, creeping plant, found in abundance along the edges of streams, stagnant ponds, and old water-ditches in this country. Quiet, shallow water supplied from springs affords the right conditions for its growth. A few years ago I was in possession of four or five acres of a fresh-water swamp, and at least one quarter of the surface was covered with Water-Cress. It will succeed best, however, when the roots are planted along the edge of a shallow running stream, with a sandy bottom. On a heavy clay bottom, it runs the risk of being more or less injured in Winter.

As it is a hardy perennial, when the roots are once started along the nooks and corners of such a stream, there can be a constant supply gathered from year to year, for home or market, according to the extent of the surface.

There is a brisk demand in market for Water-Cress; and when it first comes, early in the Spring, the prices range from fifty cents to one dollar per basket holding only three quarts. It would be difficult, indeed, to estimate the value of an acre, even at twenty cents a quart.

What reaches the market now is principally gathered from many sources by Germans, who, even collecting it in this way, in small lots, find it a profitable business.

Water-Cress comes into full bearing the second year from the time of setting out the roots. It can be propagated and a bed started by sowing the seed where it is wanted to grow permanently. But this method is not as reliable as growing the plants in a seed-bed, and then transplanting them along the edge of the water-course, about ten or twelve inches apart. Roots may be taken up from some stream or pond, when found growing, to form a new bed. In gathering it for table use or market, it should always be cut, and not pulled; the latter way disturbs and injures the roots. Two ounces of seed will give enough plants to suppy a large family.

There are three well-known varieties, but the LARGE BROWN-LEAVED is the best for this climate.

Water-Cress is frequently served as a breakfast Salad. It is very popular, having a peculiar pungent taste, that most people are fond of in a Salad.

### CHIVES, OR CIVES.

*Allium schænoprasum.*

This is a hardy perennial bulb—a species of Onion. Permanent beds of Chives are usually found in well-stocked kitchen-gardens. They grow in tufts, the leaves resembling fine rushes. The tops are cut off when green, to flavor soups and Salads, and also to be eaten in the raw state, the same as young Onions. In taste they are similar to the Onion and Leek.

Chives are propagated by dividing the roots and planting them ten or twelve inches apart each way, in April. The tops will soon begin to grow, and they should be cut off three or four times during the season. A bed well cared for will continue to produce for at least a dozen years.

### CHEVRIL.

*Scandix cerifolium.*

There are two varieties of Chevril cultivated: the Parsley and the Fern-leaved. While the leaves are young, they are used in soups and Salads, to which they impart a pleasant, aromatic flavor. In appearance they resemble the Curled Parsley.

Chevril is a hardy annual, propagated from seed, and succeeds best when sown on a deep, light, rich soil. The drills should be made one foot apart and half an inch deep. The seed, after being distributed in these drills, should be covered by raking the bed with a wooden rake, drawn in the line of the bed. It is only good while young; so that, to keep a supply, it will be necessary to have a succession of sowings once every two or three weeks, from the middle of April until the 1st of August.

The seed is small; one ounce will be enough to sow for family use.

## CHEVRIL, TURNIP-ROOTED.

*Chærophyllum bulbosum.*

This is a comparatively new vegetable, and in its habits is similar to the common Parsnip. During the excitement about the Potato-rot in Europe, it was recommended as a substitute for the Potato, and as being fully equal to it in quality. In shape it resembles the Parsnip. When boiled, it is dry, white, and farinaceous, but it tastes more like boiled Chestnuts than Potatoes.

The seed may be sown in drills in April, and cultivated like Parsnips or Carrots. On well-manured ground it will yield five or six tons to the acre. The roots may be left in the ground during Winter, or harvested and kept in pits, or in a root-cellar, until the following Spring.

### CORN.

*Zea mays.*

Sweet Corn is generally cultivated as a garden vegetable; but in some districts, where land is not very expensive, it is grown on a large scale for market. New Jersey and Long Island farmers raise annually hundreds of acres for the New York market; and, taking one year with another, Sweet Corn will pay from seventy-five to one hundred dollars per acre. The profits from this crop are not large, but the demand is usually good, and it will pay the grower about double what common field Corn will, with the same labor and expense for manure.

By proper management in the times of planting, a constant supply can easily be had from July until frost. For home use, by planting four different times, three weeks apart, commencing on the 1st of May, fresh Green Corn, for boiling, can be furnished daily from the garden.

In growing Sweet Corn for market, farmers usually make two plantings; the first one, for the early crop, which should be planted four feet apart each way, about the 1st of May, in case the weather is settled. A well-worked sandy loam is preferable for the first crop, because such kind of soil can be planted earlier, and, consequently, the corn will be ready for market sooner. Earliness is very important to those who grow corn for market. When it first comes, it will bring two to three dollars per hundred ears. As the season advances and the supply is greater, prices fall to from seventy-five cents to one dollar per hundred ears.

Before planting, the ground should be ploughed and harrowed once or twice, marked out 4 x 4, and some well-rotted manure or other compost applied in the hill, at the rate of ten or twelve two-horse loads to the acre.

The corn is then dropped and covered, putting five kernels to each hill. At the first hoeing, only three stocks should be left growing in a hill. The culture between the rows is done with a horse-cultivator, running often enough to keep down the weeds and to loosen the surface. When the Corn is planted early in May, the crop will be marketed by the middle of August, in time to sow Yellow Stone or Strapleaved Red-top Turnip. An application of three or four hundred pounds to the acre of fine bone-dust or superphosphate, at the first hoeing, will forward the date of ripening.

The second crop, intended for a late market, may be planted any time from the middle of June to the 1st of July, according to the locality.

Green Corn always rises in price again towards the close of the season. Growers know this fact, and try to avail themselves of it by planting late; but sometimes an early frost interferes with their plans.

HOWE'S HORSE-HOE.

The kinds generally grown are the following:

DARLING'S EXTRA EARLY is a popular, early market variety. The ears are not large, but close, well-formed, and very sweet.

EARLY DWARF SUGAR is a good variety for the garden. The stock is small, not more than three feet high, the ears medium-sized, and the kernels very sweet. It may be planted closer than the taller kinds; 3 x 3 will be far enough apart.

MAMMOTH SWEET is a large late variety, white cob, and large, well-formed ears, sixteen rows.

FARMERS' CLUB SWEET is a good variety for either

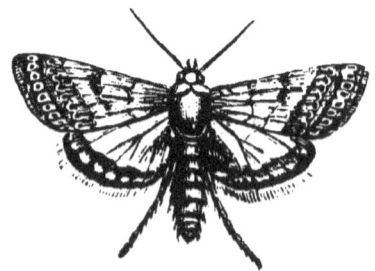

BOLL WORM.

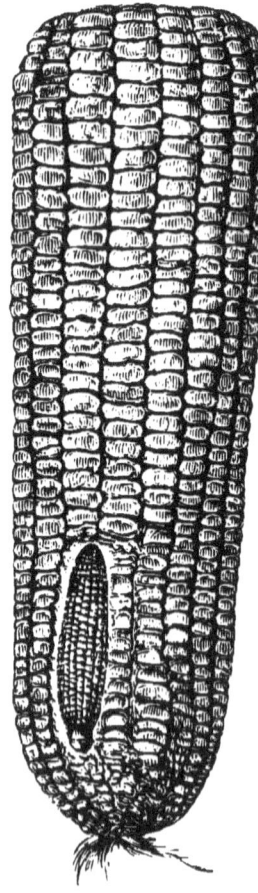

MAMMOTH SWEET.

garden-culture or market. It matures in about seventy days from the time of planting. The quality is good. It has eight rows, large kernels, and boils tender.

STOWELL'S EVERGREEN is without doubt the *best* late variety on the list. The stocks will produce from three to five ears each. The ears are of a large size, the kernels deep, frequently irregular, and very tender and sweet when boiled. This variety will remain in a green state longer than any other kind of Sweet Corn that we have grown.

The Evergreen is so liable to mix with other varieties of Corn, that it is difficult to keep it pure.

One quart of seed—of two or more of the kinds enumerated—planted in equal parts at different times, will be sufficient for a large family.

The late crop of Sweet Corn last year was seriously injured by the Southern "Boll Worm" (*Heliothis armigera*). It infested almost every ear, eating the ends, or one or two rows of kernels. When full-grown, this worm is about an inch in length, of a dark-brown color, with a light yellow stripe the length of the body on either side. The only remedy that we know of, is to make small fires near the corn-patch, in the evening, to attract the moths, and in this way destroy them before laying their eggs.

### CUCUMBER.

*Cucumis sativus.*

The Cucumber is a tender annual. It is very extensively cultivated. Early in the season it is cut into slices for a Salad, and later it is made into Pickles; in both ways it is very popular among all classes. When cut into quarters lengthwise, and tied in bunches and boiled, they make a good substitute for Asparagus.

Market-gardeners grow the Cucumber on a large scale, both under glass and in the open field. When properly managed, it will usually pay a handsome profit. Early in the season the demand is good and prices high; but, as with most other vegetables cultivated for market, earliness is all-important. Later in the Summer the demand falls off, the supply is large, and the prices are very low,

## CUCUMBERS.

The Cucumber cannot be planted out of doors with any safety until May, when the weather is settled and the ground is warm. To gain time, gardeners sow the seed in moderate hot-beds, from the 1st to the 10th of April, either in rows three inches apart, or in thumb-pots, putting three or four seeds to each pot. The seed will sprout in a week from the time of planting, and then the plants should be aired freely every day, to prevent them from growing too spindling. Early in May the ground should be prepared in the usual way. The more thoroughly pulverized the soil, the better will the result be in the crop of Cucumbers. The ground should be marked out five feet each way, and at each intersection a hole made with a spade. Into each of these holes a forkful of well-rotted manure should be put, and then fine soil drawn over this manure, forming a hill two or three inches above the level of the surface, and ten or twelve inches in diameter.

The plants in the frames by this time will have three or four rough leaves, and will be fully ready to transplant to the hills. This should be done in cloudy or damp weather, and always in the afternoon. The plants should be taken up with considerable care, so as not to disturb the roots, and three of them set in each hill. This will take a few more than five thousand plants to the acre, and they can be grown in twelve or fifteen sashes of 3 x 6.

MANURE FORK.

For garden-culture, the seed is usually sown in the hills early in May, putting eight or ten seeds in each hill. The "striped bug" (*Coreus tristis*) often destroys the young plants just as they appear above the ground. To get rid of these very troublesome little pests, we sprinkle the surface of the hills and the leaves of the plants with fine flour of bone once every two days. If this does not drive the bugs off we water the vines with the solution of tobacco, &c. (recommended for Cabbage plants), early in the morning, and then, immediately after, dust the plants with the bone or superphosphate.

As fast as the young vines grow, the earth should be drawn around the stems, for the bugs will destroy these by perforating them.

When the Cucumbers are started in a hot-bed, the vines are strong enough, when transplanted to the open field, to resist the attack of the bugs. When the vines begin to run, by pinching off the ends at the third joint, they will branch nearer the hill, forming blossoms and Cucumbers earlier than they otherwise would. If there are no drawbacks, an acre of Cucumbers—the plants started under glass—will yield from three hundred to three hundred and fifty dollars an acre. Before Cucumbers were grown so extensively at Charleston and Norfolk, the profits were much larger than they are now. On Long Island, and in some parts of New Jersey and of Westchester County, N. Y., Cucumbers are grown in large quantities for pickling. For this purpose the culture is somewhat different; the ground is ploughed once or twice in the Spring, and any time from the middle of June to the 10th of July the field is furrowed out five feet apart. The manure is strewn along these furrows, and then two furrows from either side are thrown together. The top of the ridge is levelled at intervals, four or five feet apart, and then the seed is put in. A cultivator is run frequently between the rows, but the work around the hills requires the hand-hoe. By pinching the vines at the third joint, as mentioned above, the crop will be increased. The Cucumbers are gathered every day and sent to market. A large grower on Long Island informed me that his profits average from one hundred and twenty-five to one hundred and fifty dollars per acre; when grown by contract, at one dollar and seventy-five cents per thousand.

Since the close of the war, the Cucumber is extensively grown for Northern markets around Norfolk, Va., and Charleston, S. C. The difference in climate affords special advantages for the cultivation of this crop, for profit, at the South. But at Charleston, what is gained by the climate is thrown away by the careless manner in which most of the Cucumbers coming from that point are gathered and packed. On reaching New York, they are too large, over-ripe, and yellow, and they have to be sold at very low prices.

HAND-HOE.

If the Southern gardeners would adopt the same method—starting the young plants under glass, or have small wooden boxes, with covers of glass, to protect against late frosts—that the Northern gardeners do, Cucumbers would be a profitable crop, very *much* more so than it is at present.

Charleston Cucumbers, that reach New York in good order in May, bring from seven to eight dollars per crate, holding about one hundred Cucumbers. In June the price falls to seventy-five cents or one dollar a box of the same quantity; and still later there is no demand at all for Southern Cucumbers. Growers near Charleston do not realize now, in a favorable season, more than two to three hundred dollars per acre, of which about one-half is profit. I know, however, of one instance when sixteen hundred dollars was made from a single acre of Cucumbers grown in the neighborhood of Charleston and sold in New York.

Late frosts frequently injure the young vines. In 1868 some friends in James' Island had two-thirds of their vines killed by a frost on the 3d of April, but, with the small boxes spoken of, the vines would have been saved. In field-culture the spaces between the rows should be thoroughly cultivated before the vines begin to run, and no weeds nor grass allowed to get possession of the ground.

A dozen and a half of hills, well-managed in the garden, will keep the family table well supplied during the season. An ounce of seed will plant that number of hills. It is better to plant plenty of seed, for the "*striped bug*" may destroy some; and when the vines begin to run, all but three plants to a hill may be pulled up.

The most reliable and popular varieties for field or garden-culture are the following:

EARLY RUSSIAN.—This is one of the earliest for the garden. The Cucumbers are small, but tender, and of good quality.

EARLY FRAME is one of the standard, well-known varieties, grown widely for home use, and also for market. It is larger and smoother than the Early Russian, and a few days later.

WHITE SPINE is the most popular kind among gardeners, either for forcing or out of door culture. It grows larger than the FRAME, uniformly straight,

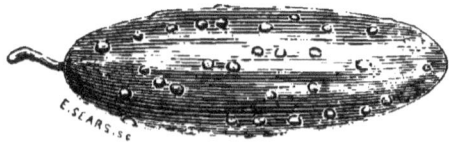

WHITE SPINE.

with more white spines. The flavor is good, flesh crisp, and it will keep better than any other variety grown for market.

LONG GREEN PRICKLY is one of the long-growing sorts. When full-grown, it will average twelve inches in length. The flesh is firm and brittle. It is only grown for home use or for pickles.

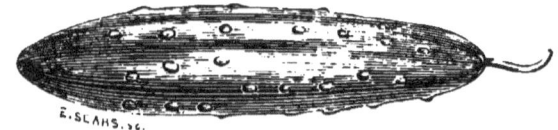

LONG GREEN PRICKLY.

None of the long-growing kinds of Cucumbers

are favorites in market, although many of them are of fine quality.

GHERKIN, OR WEST INDIAN, is a small, oval-shaped, prickly Cucumber, used exclusively for pickles. It is a late variety. It does not grow longer than two or three inches. It is full of seeds. The vines are rank growers, and need plenty of room.

Full directions for forcing Cucumbers under glass will be found under the headings "Hot-Beds" and "Forcing-Houses," in another part of this work. Also detailed accounts about the expense of constructing such houses as are now being built by gardeners near New York, and other large Northern cities.

# CHAPTER VI.

### EGG PLANT.

*Solanum melongena.*

This plant is a native of Africa and Tropical America. In some sections it is known as Quince Squash. It is very generally cultivated in this country, and highly esteemed for culinary purposes.

Egg Plants are not grown in large quantities by our market-gardeners, but they usually pay handsomely to the extent that it is safe to grow them for market. Those who are engaged largely in this branch of industry, and favorably situated, seldom plant more than an acre of Egg Plants; it would be considered a large piece of ground to devote to this vegetable.

The Egg Plant is a tender annual, more difficult to start in the Spring than any other kind of vegetable we grow. It requires more bottom-heat, and for a longer time, than the other kinds of seeds that are started in hot-beds.

We sow the seed in drills, three inches apart, in hot-beds, from the 16th to the 20th of March, and, when the plants are two inches high, transplant them into another bed, two inches apart each way. Both in the seed-bed and transplanting-bed the sashes should be protected with straw mats at night, until the weather is settled and warm.

While the plants are young, the sashes should not be opened to admit air until an hour or two after the removal of the mats; if this is neglected, the plants will "damp off," and very often all the first sowing is lost in this way.

IMPROVED NEW YORK EGG PLANT.

The seed should be of the previous year's growth, although seed two years old will germinate; fresh seed is better. One ounce of seed will give at least one thousand plants, and a small package will be enough for family use. (For more detailed directions for forcing Egg Plants, see chapter on Hot-Beds.)

When the plants have been treated as directed (for the latitude of New York), they may be transplanted into the open ground by the 20th of May. They require a deep, rich soil, well worked. We set the plants three feet apart each way, and sprinkle some superphosphate or some finely-ground bone immediately around the roots at the time of planting. Each plant is taken from the bed with a square of earth around the roots. The afternoon before transplanting, the plants are copiously watered, so that the soil will adhere to the roots. Then, with a long-bladed knife to cut through on either side, each plant is removed without disturbing the roots. The plants are placed on a wheel-barrow, and taken where they are to be set out.

It is important to use all this care, for, unless all the conditions are just right, Egg Plants are very tardy in starting, and with the market-gardener this is a matter of dollars and cents. When they first come into market they usually bring two dollars per dozen; later, the price goes down to seventy-five cents or one dollar a dozen.

The ground should be hoed frequently, kept loose and free from weeds. Plants that grow to full size will average from seven to nine eggs to a plant, of the "New York Improved." Two or three dozen plants will give an abundance of eggs for a family of six or eight persons.

VARIETIES.—There are four or five kinds of Egg Plants, but only one or two are worthy of cultivation for market.

NEW YORK IMPROVED.—With an experience in

growing Egg Plants for market for fifteen years, this variety is the most reliable and productive of any that we have cultivated. The plants are vigorous in their habits of growth, seldom, if ever, failing to produce a crop of fruit, of a deep purple color, uniformly large, and, when cooked, of good quality.

BLACK PEKIN is a new variety. The plant grows more erect than the "Improved." The foliage and branches are of a rich purple color, making an ornamental plant, and, at the same time, producing abundant fruit. The eggs are a very dark purple, nearly black, of large size and good quality. This variety is worthy of trial for market as well as for the kitchen-garden.

WHITE EGG PLANT is grown principally for ornamental purposes. The fruit, when full-grown, is long, egg-shaped, and of a pure white color.

LONG PURPLE was at one time grown for market, but compared with the "New York Improved," it has not with us given anything like the same number of eggs to the plant. The fruit is long, purple in color, and of fair quality.

### HOW TO SAVE EGG PLANT SEED.

The market-gardener will always make it a rule to select from his crop a few specimens, the best of their kind for his seed, the following year. When this plan is faithfully carried out, there is no fear that this home-saved seed will not come up, under ordinary circumstances; and when it does come up, the variety is sure to be true to name, which is not always the case when the seeds are bought from venders or from irresponsible seedsmen. There is nothing more vexatious in the gardener's legitimate routine of business, than to make all the necessary preparations for seed—preparing the ground with care, manuring, &c., &c.,—and then to find out, after it is too late to make a second attempt, that the seed is old and it will not germinate, or that instead of Cauliflower, the plants are mixed varieties of Cabbage.

The largest and best formed eggs should be reserved for seed and to separate the seed from the flesh requires some skill and care. For doing this work, choose a bright, clear day, and begin the work early in the morning, so that the seeds can be separated and partly dried before the sun goes down. If not, the whole lot may be rendered worthless by sprouting during the night.

Although so hard to start in the hot-bed, when first washed out from the eggs it sprouts more easily than any other kind of garden-seed. We have had large quantities, at different times, spoiled in this way, in a single night.

The eggs should first be peeled, and then the part of the stem end that contains no seeds cut off. The balance is cut into small pieces and thrown into a tub or pail of water. Each of these pieces is then taken in the hand and tightly squeezed; this displaces the seed from the flesh, and when all the seed is separated in this way, the pulp is thrown away. The good seed will settle at the bottom of the vessel, and by slowly pouring the water from one tub to another, all the extraneous matter can easily be removed, leaving the seed clean. Before passing the water from tub to tub, it may sometimes be found necessary to rub between the hands those portions of the pulp, to which some of the seeds may still adhere. This may be separated from the seed by pouring the contents of the vessel through a sieve, with a mesh large enough for the seed to pass out, while it retains a large part of the pulp.

When the seed is freed from the pulp it should at once be placed on a fine sieve, or on a board, with a smooth surface, spread out thinly and set in the sun to dry. It should be stirred frequently during the day, say every half hour, so that the surface of the seed will be hardened enough not to sprout during the night. It will require a couple of days' exposure to dry the seed, and when sufficiently dry it should be put into a bag and hung up in a garret or seed-room until wanted.

KEEPING EGG PLANTS.—When the fruit is wanted for winter use the eggs should be taken from the vines in November, or earlier, that is, before being touched by the frost. For a few weeks, until the weather grows colder, they will keep on a barn floor, or under a shed, where they are sheltered. Later in the season, when severe cold weather sets in, the sound specimens should be placed on shelves in a dry, cool, cellar. With this treatment Egg Plants can be kept in good condition for the table until the first of January.

Market gardeners, who have plenty of frames, often start Egg Plants under glass, early in the season, and force the plants so as to have the fruit early. Two plants to a sash, either in a forcing-pit or spent hot-bed, will be enough, and the fruit may be ready for market a month earlier. They bring from four to five dollars per dozen when grown in this way.

The demand is, of course, limited. Early Egg Plants, grown at Norfolk and Charleston, and shipped north would pay very well to a limited extent.

## ENDIVE.

### *Cichorium endivia.*

Endive is but little used in this country except by Germans and French, who consume it freely in the Fall and early Winter in flavoring soups and making salads. It is a hardy annual; the seed may be sown in the open ground any time from April until the first of August. The crop will mature in about ninety days from the time of sowing. For the Fall crop the seed should be sown in drills, twelve inches apart and a quarter of an inch deep, early in July. When the plants are up a scuffle-hoe should be run between the rows occasionally, to keep down the weeds. By the middle of August the first planting may be made, setting the plants one foot apart each way, on any kind of ground that is loose and rich. The cultivation needed is to keep the spaces clean between the plants with the common garden hoe.

When the plants attain their full size the leaves are long and spreading. This vegetable is only in demand when the "hearts" are bleached. To do this the outside leaves are gathered up in a bunch and fastened in this way, with a small quantity of straw, hay, or bass matting. By thus excluding the light, the inside leaves will change color to a yellowish white. It will take from fourteen to sixteen days for this change to take place in mild weather; a few days longer will be required later in the season, when the weather is colder. A smart workman will tie up six hundred or seven hundred heads in a day.

Any means by which the light can be excluded will bring about the same result, and if old shingles are abundant, a few laid on top of each head will answer the purpose. English gardeners sometimes draw the soil around Endive in the same way as for bleaching Celery; this, however, is tedious and much more expensive.

A small paper of seed will be enough to sow for family use.

When seed is wanted the sowing should be made early in April and the transplanting a month or so later, leaving more space between the rows. When the seed stock starts to grow it should be tied to a stake driven along side. The seed should be gathered as fast as it ripens; it does not all ripen at the same time. Three or four strong plants will yield an abundant supply.

VARIETIES.—Of these there are three or four known to gardeners. The best, either for the main crop for market or for home use, is the

GREEN CURLED.—It is decidedly the best variety for cultivation, being less affected by sudden changes of the weather than the other kinds. When bleached, it is quite an ornamental plant, and the most popular with consumers, as it is very tender and crisp.

BROAD-LEAVED BATAVIA grows larger, requiring

more room than the Curled. It is only used in stews and soups, being also very much inferior in quality.

French Moss is a very fine curled variety. When more generally known, it will be a favorite on account of its appearance, texture, and quality.

When Endive is well bleached in the Fall, we usually get from seventy-five cents to one dollar per dozen heads from German grocers, who always keep a supply on hand. The demand, however, is limited.

## Garlic.

### *Allium sativum.*

The Garlic came originally from Sicily. The kind cultivated in the gardens of this country is a hardy perennial. It is grown somewhat extensively; but it is used principally by French and Germans for flavoring soups, stews, and salads. It imparts a strong, and to most Americans, an unpleasant taste; and eaten in a concentrated form, taints the breath of the person who uses it. Two varieties are grown, the large and the small. The bulb, which is enclosed in a thin, white skin, divides into parts or cloves. These divisions are planted in the Spring in drills, one foot apart, and the cloves two inches deep and six inches apart in the rows.

When planted in April, the crop can be gathered about the middle of August and stored like Onions. The demand in market is not large, but Garlic will pay about as well as Onions to the extent that there is a call for it.

One quart of the "sets" will yield an abundant

supply for family use. They will make the largest bulbs when planted on a light, rich loam, and kept well cultivated while growing.

### HORSE-RADISH.
#### *Cochlearia armoracia.*

Horse-Radish is an important crop with market-gardeners near large cities, and when grown on rich deep ground is profitable. In Essex and Hudson counties, New Jersey, and in Kings and Queens counties, New York, Horse-Radish is extensively cultivated for New York markets. It is always planted by these growers as a second crop, following Early Cabbages or Beets. When planted between these, the "sets" are put out, two feet one way and eighteen inches the other. At these distances it will take about fifteen thousand roots to plant an acre.

The Cabbages and Beets are planted early in April, just as soon as the ground is dry enough to be worked. The Horse-Radish "sets" are planted

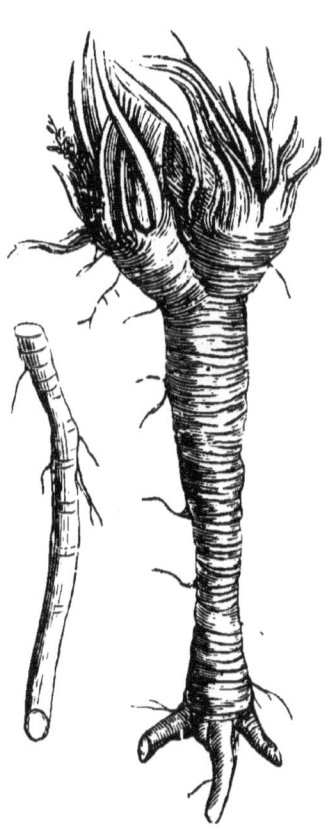

HORSE-RADISH ROOT

a month later, in the following manner. One man is provided with a light crowbar, with which he makes a hole about ten or eleven inches deep between every two Cabbages all along the line. Another man follows with a bundle of the roots, drops one in each hole and fills in the earth around it, with a "dibble," having the top of the set about two inches below the surface.

When preparing these sets in the Fall,—leaving them six or seven inches long—the tops should be cut off square and the lower end of the root slanting, so that when planting, in the Spring, no mistake will be made, putting them in upside down.

By the time the Beets, Cauliflowers or Cabbages are marketed, the Horse-Radish will be well above ground. In case the roots start quickly, making too much growth before the first crops have been taken from the ground, we chop off the tops with the hoe, without injuring the after growth, in the least. As soon as the early crop is removed, the ground is well cultivated, keeping the surface loose and free from weeds through August, September and October, for this crop will make all its growth in these three months. The tops are so large and spreading that there is very little trouble in cultivating Horse-Radish, as it is now grown by market-gardeners near New York and other large Northern cities. The old-fashioned method of allowing the roots to remain in the ground two years, has been abandoned by the modern gardener as useless and unnecessary: for when planted in the way described, in rich soil, the roots will attain full size in a single year.

This is but one of the many improvements introduced by the modern market-gardener, in cultivating vegetables for profit, over the old style private gardeners, who have always been opposed to such *innovations.*

In the latter part of November, the roots will have attained their full growth and they can then be dug and stored for Winter use. At the time of digging, it is not unusual to have many of the roots weigh two pounds a piece. Before pitting, the tops are cut off and all the straggling small roots are trimmed off. These small roots are carefully preserved for "sets" for the next year's planting. The large roots that are intended for market, are then put into pits. A spot is selected where there is a natural descent for the water, three feet wide and as long as may be required. First, a layer of the roots is put down, then a thin layer of earth, and so alternate layers are added, until the pit is three or four feet high. Then the whole is covered with earth, eight or ten inches deep. The roots of Horse-Radish are not injured by frost. The alternate layers of earth will keep the roots from heating and in such a position that they can be taken out at any time during the Winter, when the demand and prices satisfy the grower.

The small roots, intended for next year's use, may be put into narrow trenches, as described for Celery, until wanted in the Spring, when they are cut the proper length for planting.

The price of Horse-Radish varies from year to year. In the Fall of 1869 it was only worth seven cents per pound, while in the following February, the same quality of roots sold for eighteen cents per pound. At present, large, well-grown roots are worth from ten to twelve dollars per hundred pounds. On very rich ground and under the most favorable circumstances, from four to five tons of Horse-Radish are produced on an acre. But the average yield, obtained by most growers, does not equal this amount. Three or four tons to the acre may be considered a fair crop, and when sold at from one hundred to one hundred and thirty dollars per ton, it would pay a handsome profit, from the fact of its easy culture.

The method of preparing Horse-Radish for market, is simple and rapid. The roots are taken from the pit to the market-house—the tops and small roots having been trimmed off in the Fall—thrown into a large wash-tub and with the aid of a scrubbing-brush thoroughly cleaned. In this state the roots are sent to market. For the kitchen-garden, it is well to adopt the same method of cultivation. Twenty sets planted every Spring will yield enough to supply a family.

As soon as the crop of Horse-Radish is taken out of the ground in the Fall, the bed or field should be ploughed. This will displace and expose to view nearly all of the smaller roots that were left in the ground at the time of digging. It is well to have a boy follow the plough and gather all of these roots, for if left undisturbed for a single season, it will be found a troublesome task to get rid of the Horse-Radish. By following this plan, very few of these small roots will be left in the ground, and any that still remain can be taken out when the ground is again ploughed in the Spring, before planting with another crop.

## KOHL-RABI.

*Brassica caulo-rapa.*

The Kohl-Rabi or Turnip-rooted Cabbage is not generally known or cultivated in this country. It is evidently a hybrid between the Cabbage and Turnip, and to some extent partakes of the characteristics of both.

For early use, we sow the seed in a hot-bed about

KOHL-RABI.

the middle of March, transplant once, into another bed in April and plant in the open ground early in May. When the Kohl-Rabi is two-thirds grown, if boiled and sliced, it will be found tender, more delicate in flavor, than either Cabbage or Turnip and not unlike Cauliflower.

There is a limited demand in market, for those grown early, by the Germans and French, who prize them highly. In preparing them for market, the stems are cut off close to the bulb and three of them tied by the leaves in a bunch. They bring from seventy-five cents to one dollar per dozen bunches, and to the extent of the demand for them, pay very well at these prices. As a late crop or for a succession, the seed is sown in the open ground in the same way as Cabbage-seed—about the 10th of May, and a second sowing may be made a month later.

When the plants are three or four inches high, they are transplanted; two feet between the rows and one foot apart in the row. Like all the Cabbage tribe, they will grow best on deep, rich soil. It is stated by some that the Kohl-Rabi is difficult to transplant, we have grown it for many years, and never found this to be the case, no more difficult than Cabbage plants.

The ground between the rows should be kept constantly stirred while the plants are growing and no weeds suffered to remain. A small paper of seed will give enough plants to stock the kitchen-garden. In order to have them young and tender for the table, two or three plantings should be made during the season. For cooking, they should not be allowed to grow full size, if they do, the outside skin becomes hard and tough.

Sooner or later, the Kohl-Rabi will be cultivated on a large scale, in the stock-growing districts of this country for feeding cattle during the winter. In field culture they are more easily grown than the

Ruta Baga and they yield a larger weight of roots to the acre than Turnips. The ground should be prepared and ridged, as directed for Carrots, and the seed sown on these drills, using one and a half pounds of fresh seed to the acre. They should be treated in every way like Turnips, the only difference being, that they should not be left standing quite as thick in the rows. Eight or ten inches apart will be found close enough. The leaves of the Kohl-Rabi are equally valuable for feeding purposes as the roots. One bushel of these roots is worth nearly two bushels of the common White Turnip, for cattle, and they are fully equal, if not superior, to the best Ruta Baga. The seed should be sown in July, and the roots can be pitted in the Fall in the same way as Turnips, Carrots, or Beets.

Or, the seed can be sown in a seed-bed and transplanted if more convenient. Although for field-culture we prefer sowing the seed in place, and thinning out the plants to the proper distance apart.

VARIETIES.—There are only two kinds of Kohl-Rabi, that are grown to any extent.

EARLY WHITE.—This is the best variety, both for the kitchen-garden and market. It is of a glossy white color, flesh tender while young, and good for the table when the bulbs are three or four inches in diameter.

EARLY PURPLE —This variety is in every way similar to the White except in color, which the name designates. For table use, it is just as good, but it does not sell as well in market, on account of the color.

The Green and Large Purple varieties are coarser in flesh, they are only grown for cattle feeding. The bulbs attain a larger size than the first two sorts named.

# CHAPTER VII.

## LETTUCE.

### *Lactuca sativa.*

THE Lettuce is a hardy annual and one of the most generally cultivated and popular vegetables in the Catalogue. It is very healthful as a Spring and Summer salad; for this purpose it is unequalled. It may be divided into two classes, the Cabbage or Head Lettuce, and the upright growing sorts from the Island of Cos, known as the Cos Lettuce. To have the latter kind in perfection, the leaves should be tied up as recommended for Endive, and blanched. When treated in this way, the leaves are tender, crisp and delicate.

The Cabbage, or Head sorts, are now extensively cultivated, both for family use and by the market-gardener, who looks upon this crop as easily cultivated, and profitable. This is especially so if the location of his garden is within easy distance from a large market, so as to deliver the Lettuce with his own wagon to the huckster or grocer.

The Lettuce is grown on a large scale for market, in the open field, planted usually between rows of Early Cabbages, putting the Lettuce plants from fifteen to eighteen inches apart in the row, and alternate with the rows of Cabbages, which leaves the distance between the rows two feet. This arrangement will give from fifteen thousand to seventeen thousand heads of Lettuce to an acre. The Lettuce crop will be ready for market and sold before the Cabbages require all the room. When there are fifteen thousand planted on good ground, twelve thousand of them will be marketable and they will bring from seven dollars and fifty cents to ten dollars per thousand heads.

The seed for this early crop is sown in the Fall, from the 5th to the 10th of September, in the open ground. About the middle of October, we transplant into cold frames, putting six or eight hundred plants to a sash of 3 x 6. The winter treatment is similar to that recommended for keeping Cabbage plants. During cold weather, the beds are covered with sashes, giving air in very mild or warm weather.

For family use, a small quantity of seed may be sown at the same date. A rough structure of boards may be fixed for protecting the plants during the Winter; or if the seed is sown in a sheltered spot in the garden and mulched before cold weather sets in, with salt hay or other litter, the plants will keep fresh until Spring, when they can be transplanted.

Again, for the kitchen-garden, a small paper of seed, sown in a hot-bed, about the first of March, will give plants large enough to set out in the open ground in the latter part of April. To have a succession of plantings, more seed can be sown in the open ground in April and transplanted to the garden; the Lettuce will come to maturity in six weeks from the time of planting.

# LETTUCE.

When Lettuce is set out in a bed by itself, the plants may be put fifteen inches apart each way. Like most other garden products, it needs, in order to insure success, a deep, rich soil that is kept well cultivated.

Growing Lettuce in Winter, by bottom-heat, both in hot-beds and in forcing-pits, is a large and lucrative branch of the market-gardener's business, when situated near large cities. Formerly a large part of the frame Lettuce was grown in cold-beds; planted in November (fifty plants to a sash), the crop would be ready for market early in May. This system has given way, in turn, to hot-beds and, more recently, to forcing-houses, put up expressly for growing vegetables (especially Lettuce) during the Winter months. There have been a dozen or more of this kind of *house* put up in the vicinity of Newark, N. J., last year, and as many more will be built the present season. Considering the economy of time in managing these forcing-houses, they will, without doubt, entirely supersede the old style hot-bed system.

Under the headings "Hot-Beds" and "Forcing-Houses," there will be found fuller directions about their care, construction, &c., &c.

Although there is a long list of varieties of Lettuce given in seedsmen's catalogues, only a few of them will pay to grow either for family use or market. Among the best for either purpose may be named

EARLY CURLED SIMPSON.—This is one of the best curled varieties now cultivated. It is superior to the

Curled Silesia and more reliable for field-culture. It has been grown extensively in cold frames, but it is not a good variety for forcing with bottom-heat. It is grown, in preference to any other, by market-gardeners, for a Spring crop among Cabbages and Cauliflowers. It is an excellent kind for Spring planting in the kitchen-garden.

TENNIS BALL.—This variety forms a small, solid head, and is a very superior kind for forcing-purposes, for which it is extensively used. The leaves are nearly smooth, and, when full grown, the head is tender, juicy, and crisp.

BOSTON HEAD LETTUCE.—The variety known to gardeners by this name is a white-seeded butter. The leaves are smooth. It forms a head one quarter larger than the TENNIS BALL, and is a reliable kind for forcing. It is popular in market on account of its size and quality.

BLACK SEEDED BUTTER forms a large head when planted in the open ground in Spring; it will not stand bottom-heat, and it is, therefore of very little use for forcing. But it is extensively grown in the garden and field, and is one of the most profitable for this purpose.

BROWN DUTCH is a hardy sort, that will stand the Winter better than other kinds that we grow.

LARGE INDIAN grows large in the open ground, and stands the Summer heat better than any other of the good varieties. It has a curled leaf, lighter in color than the Silesia, and is a popular Summer kind.

PARIS GREEN COS.—This variety of the Cos is

the best for culture in this country. It has an upright growth, with long, narrow leaves. These should be fastened up with a little straw, for ten or twelve days before cutting, to blanch. With this treatment, the Cos will be found of superior quality for salads.

Gardeners should not overlook the importance of selecting the best specimens of their kinds of Lettuce, to grow for seed. To plant seeds not true to name is an unprofitable business.

A hundred plants planted every month in the Spring will afford enough for family use. A small paper each of two varieties will, when sown in a sheltered spot in the garden, give that number of plants.

## LEEK.

*Allium porrum.*

The Leek is a hardy biennial, that will stand the severity of our Winters with but slight protection. It attains its full size the first year, but does not produce seed until the second. The Leek is similar in quality to the Onion; by many persons it is preferred on account of its milder flavor. It is used in soups and salads; sometimes it is boiled alone and served like Asparagus or Onions.

With the market-gardener, the Leek is always grown as a second crop; it should be cultivated in the same way by the private gardener.

The seed should be sown in a well-prepared bed, about the middle of April, in rows one foot apart.

164   LEEK.

When the plants are up, the spaces between the rows should be frequently disturbed, to prevent the

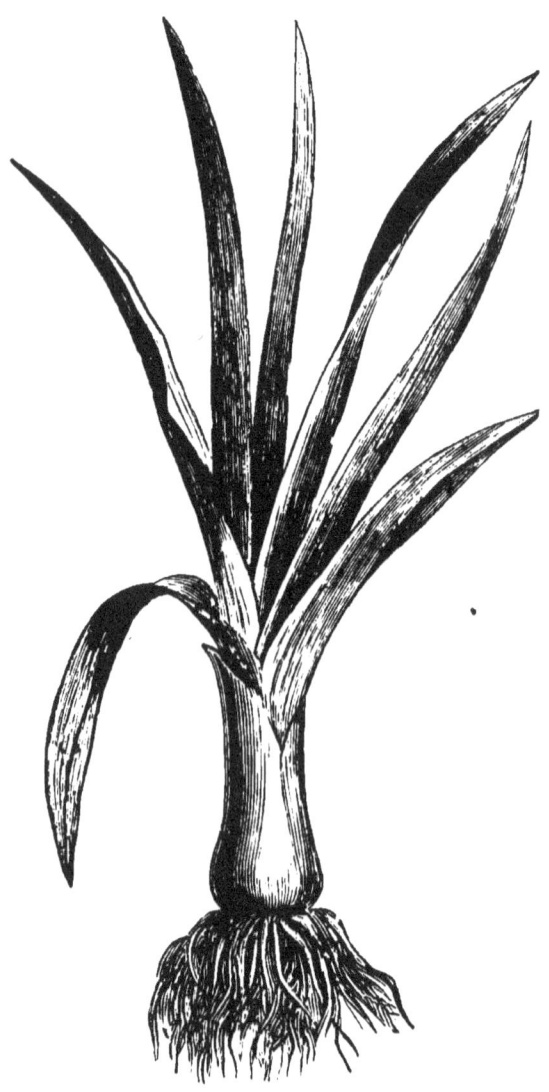

LONDON FLAG.

weeds getting any headway. By the middle of July to the first of August, when Early Potatoes, Peas, and Cabbages are removed, the ground is prepared for the Leeks.

When everything is in order and the weather favorable, the young plants are pulled and transplanted in rows one foot apart, and six inches apart in the row. The roots and leaves may be trimmed off a little at the time of transplanting. The only care necessary, from the time of setting out the plants until the Fall, is to keep the soil loose and free from weeds.

In November the Leeks may be dug up and stored, until wanted for use, in trenches similar to those described for Celery, which can be opened at all times, without much trouble.

The principal demand for Leeks, in market, is during the Winter and Spring. They usually sell freely, giving a profit of two hundred and fifty dollars to three hundred dollars per acre.

In preparing them for market, nearly all the roots and part of the tops are cut off, then washed and tied in bunches—about six large roots to a bunch.

There are only two varieties grown to any extent in this country: THE LONDON FLAG and MUSLENBURGH They are both good, very little if any preference can be given to either. For seed, some of the best roots should be kept and set out the following Spring.

Those who do not want the trouble of transplanting, can sow the seed in a permanent bed and then thin out the plants in the rows to the distance named. By this method, however, the Leeks will not attain as large a size as when transplanted.

Leek-seed can only be relied on for two years; older than this it is uncertain. An ounce of seed will be an abundance for the garden; if fresh, it will give from two thousand to three thousand plants.

## MARTYNIA.

*Martynia proboscidea.*

The Martynia is not generally cultivated by American gardeners. It is an annual. The pods are used principally for pickling.

MARTYNIA.

The plant is spreading in its habits; it should not be planted closer than two and a half feet apart each way. The seeds may be sown in a bed in April and transplanted in place the latter part of May or early in June; or they may be sown in a permanent place and thinned out when the plants are three or four inches high.

The pods are produced in great abundance; they should be used while young and tender.

## CHAPTER VIII.

MELONS.

*Cucumis melo.*

The Musk Melon is well known and is in very general cultivation in all the thickly settled parts of our country. Wherever the best varieties are grown a more extended culture of them is sure to follow. With a climate and soil so well adapted to the growth of Melons of a fine quality, it is an easy matter, for any one who owns or cultivates a piece of ground, to have, in their season, an abundant supply of this fruit.

There is a good demand for Melons in all large towns or cities, and hundreds of acres of the light soils of New Jersey and Long Island are devoted to the growth of this crop for New York markets.

When grown as a field crop, Melons seldom pay a profit of more than from seventy-five to one hundred dollars per acre. But the expense of growing is much less than that of other garden crops, and as they carry well long distances, they are usually grown on land too poor for legitimate market gardening. Within the past few years, gardeners or farmers around Norfolk, Va., and in the State of Delaware, have grown Melons on a large scale and shipped them to Northern markets, with profits ranging from fifty to one hundred dollars an acre.

In cultivating Melons, either in the kitchen-garden or for market, earliness in maturing is desirable, and any practicable means that may be available to hurry forward the ripening of the fruit, is worthy of attention. The vines while young, are in danger of being destroyed by the well-known *striped bug*. The best plan is to start the seeds in a moderate hot-bed, at the same date and treat them in the same way as directed for Cucumbers. When transplanted in place, if attacked by the bugs, apply the same remedies.

The Melon will thrive best on a deep, sandy loam, thoroughly worked. Before making the hills, the ground should be worked over twice, if in the field, with the plow, if in the garden, with the digging-fork.

The piece of ground should then be marked out, five feet apart each way. A hole is made at each intersection, with a spade, a forkful of well-rotted manure is thrown into each hole, and a hill made over this manure of the fine surface soil. The hill should be two inches higher than the surrounding surface and twelve or fifteen inches in diameter. A dozen seeds are then planted in a circle on each hill, and covered about a quarter of an inch. When the plants have formed two rough leaves, thin out, leaving only three plants to a hill. When these begin to run, pinch them back twice, to the third joint.

When the plants are started in a hot-bed, they should be lifted and set out in the same way as Cucumbers.

Twenty-five hills will yield an abundance of Melons for family use. One ounce of seed will be enough to plant this number of hills.

The ground must be well cultivated both ways with a cultivator, and around the plants, hoed two or three times with a hand-hoe. At the first hoeing, draw some earth around the stems, to support them against strong winds.

When the seed is sown in the hill, a conical wooden box, open at the top or covered with a light of glass, will be found a protection against the bugs, as well as a means of hastening the growth.

By making a square hole for the manure, twenty inches deep, then putting on top of it two or three inches of soil, which will leave the seeds when planted three inches below the level of the surface—and placing over the top of this square opening a light of glass, a forcing-bed is formed in the garden, which will be at once simple and effective as well as useful to keep off the bugs.

GARDEN SPADE.

It is not easy for the private gardener to keep Melon-seed pure. It is so liable to sport with Cucumbers or other varieties of the same family when growing in the same garden.

The best kinds for garden or field-culture are as follows:

GREEN CITRON.—Fruit medium size, nearly round.

Flesh green, thick and of good quality. The surface is roughly netted, when pure. It is a popular market variety.

NUTMEG is an old and favorite variety. It grows larger than the Citron, but is not quite so productive. The skin is dark green and netted; shape globular, flesh a light green, juicy and melting.

SKILLMAN'S FINE-NETTED is an early small-sized variety. The skin is roughly netted, the flesh green and of excellent quality.

WHITE JAPAN.—This variety, a native of Japan, is early, thin skinned, deeply ribbed, and of a light color. The flesh is thick, melting and fine flavored.

## MELON, WATER.

*Cucurbita citrullus.*

The culture of the Water Melon is essentially the same as that of the Musk Melon; the only difference being, that the Water Melon should be planted at a distance of eight feet apart each way, and in making the hills twice the quantity of manure recommended for the Musk Melon should be put to each hill.

The Water Melon will do best on new ground, where the brush has just been removed and the surface grubbed or plowed. Then by making holes, eight feet apart each way, putting in a couple of shovelfuls of compost—made of yard-manure and leaf-mould—in each hole, then making a hill over the manure and planting six or seven seeds to a hill, the yield will be satisfactory.

When the plants are fairly above the surface

they require close watching. The "striped bug" makes short work of a field of Melons, if not checked in time.

A supply of finely-ground flour of bone should be kept on hand, the surface of the hills dusted with it before the plants come through and afterward, at short intervals, until such time as the plants are past danger.

Not more than three vines should be allowed to a hill. Water Melon growers in New Jersey calculate on a profit of about one hundred dollars or one hundred and fifty dollars per acre—for a successful year. Like the Musk Melon, they will flourish best on soil of a light character, when well manured in the hill.

Two ounces of seed will be enough to plant for family use, and if convenient, it is best to start the seeds in a hot-bed. The best kinds to grow are—

MOUNTAIN SWEET.—It is one of the best for general culture. Large size, dark green color, thin rind and flesh delicious.

MOUNTAIN SPROUT is another good variety—extensively cultivated in New Jersey for market. It is a long Melon, striped lengthwise, flesh bright scarlet and of good quality.

ORANGE.—When the rind is removed from this Melon, it divides easily in sections like an Orange. It grows only medium size, oval shaped, flesh red and not first quality.

PERSIAN is a new variety, lately introduced. The form globular; color, pale green with dark stripes; flesh crimson and of good quality. It is but little known as yet, but it will be of value on account of its good keeping qualities.

CITRON.—This variety is grown exclusively for preserves. It is round, skin smooth and striped; flesh light-colored and solid.

## MUSTARD.

*Sinapis alba. Sinapis nigra.*

There are two varieties usually grown; the White Mustard cultivated for salads, and the common Brown, that is cultivated for the seed which is ground for table Mustard.

When grown in the garden, the seed may be sown thickly, in the open ground, early in April, in rows one foot apart, in loose, mellow ground. To have a succession, the sowings may be made every two or three weeks until September. Mustard must be cut for use while young, for when the leaves are full-grown, the strong flavor is unpleasant.

The Brown Mustard is grown as a field crop for the seed, for grinding. The seed may be sown in drills or broadcast, in the latter part of April or early in May, using from four to six quarts of seed to an acre. In August the crop will be ready for cutting, when it is dried and thrashed out.

When once sown in this way on a piece of ground, it is difficult to get rid of the Mustard; it is quite an annoyance, on this account.

## MUSHROOMS.

*Agaricus campestris.*

The consumption of Mushrooms in this country has very materially increased within the past dozen years, and it will probably continue to do so steadily from year to year. The supply of fresh Mushrooms has always fallen short of the demand, and yet there have been very few attempts made, so far, by men of capital to erect suitable structures for their cultivation.

The few Mushrooms that reach the markets at present are gathered in small lots in pasture fields. Occasionally, an energetic gardener, who has some unoccupied space near his boilers either in forcing or green-houses, puts up a rough contrivance for a Mushroom-bed. If successful, they are sent to market, sure to command a good price; but very often the experiment fails, and nothing more is heard of the undertaking. When a proper building can be had, and an even temperature kept up, Mushrooms may be grown for family use or for market without much trouble, provided proper care is observed in the selection and preparation of the manure used, which is the important point.

Some few years ago we constructed two caves, each five hundred feet long, for growing Mushrooms. They were fourteen feet wide, five feet deep, and covered with a board roof, forming a right angle with the two sides. The roof, made of joist for rafters and hemlock boards, was covered with earth to the depth of twenty inches and then thatched with straw. In these structures an even temperature was maintained without fire, and while the roofing lasted, the growth of Mushrooms proved a success. When the beds came into full bearing they presented an interesting sight—the entire surface of the beds dotted with the white Mushrooms that had sprung from beneath the light covering of soil in a single night. When these were gathered others were ready to take their place; and the next morning there would be the same profuse display, which was continued from week to week.

The conditions brought about by covering hemlock boards with earth soon rotted the rafters, and the roof began to fall in, which forced us to abandon the project.

There was no difficulty in finding a market for large quantities; at times in the Winter we frequently sold them at one dollar a quart to hotels and first-class eating-houses.

In preparing these caves, the object was to get all that was required for the best growth of the Mushroom—namely, darkness, and a moderate but even temperature of from forty-five to sixty degrees. It is not necessary to construct a cave for this purpose; if these conditions can be had in a house, cellar, or part of a green-house, Mushrooms can be produced in abundance, by following the directions about collecting and preparing the manure.

PREPARING MANURE.—The best manure is horse-droppings, gathered from stables where straw is used for bedding, but free from long straw. Sawdust, salt, hay, and rags are unfriendly to the growth of Mushrooms. As fast as these droppings are collected, they should be put in a heap four feet wide, four feet high, and as long as required. This heap should be made under cover. In a few days the manure will begin to heat; this should be allowed to go on until it reaches one hundred and ten degrees to one hundred and fifteen degrees, as indicated by a thermometer when the bulb is placed six or eight inches below the surface. Then tramp the manure down firmly which will always reduce the temperature. When cooled by this compression down to eighty degrees, the heap should be turned over with forks, putting the bottom and sides of the heap well into the centre, forming a heap of the same size. In case the manure looks dry, it may be wet some with a watering-pot at the time of turning. The heat in

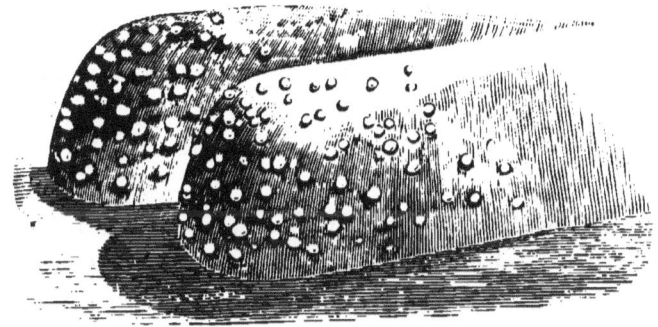

MUSHROOM-BED.

this heap will soon increase again to one hundred and ten degrees, when it should be once more tramped and turned over, forming a new heap. This may be permitted to remain without tramping until the temperature comes down to ninety degrees; if it does not in two days from the time of the last turning it must be again treated as above; when at ninety degrees it is ready to be put in place.

MAKING THE BED.—The beds should be three feet wide at the bottom and two feet and a half high, cone-shaped. The manure is taken up in large handfuls and pressed into masses of four or five inches in diameter; these are put in place and pressed firmly against each other until the bed is formed—the increase is by the addition of separate tiers. The sides of the bed are then beaten slightly with the back of a common spade, leaving the surface smooth and compact. In a day or two the manure will take heat; if it goes above ninety degrees before putting in the seed it should be allowed to cool off, which it will in a few days.

A light coating of fine garden soil is then put over the whole bed, about half an inch in thickness. The earth should be passed through a sieve before using, so as to remove lumps, stones, roots, &c., &c., and then patted down with a spade to make the surface smooth.

SPAWN.—Mushroom spawn can be bought at most horticultural stores. It usually comes in pieces of the shape and size of an ordinary brick. These bricks should be broken into pieces the size of walnuts. By means of a garden "dibble" holes are made on either side of the bed every six inches, in the direction of the length, commencing eight inches from the floor. A piece of the spawn is put into each of these holes, coming in close contact with the manure, and covered over with earth, or it may be put in before the earth is put on. Two other lines of holes are made at corresponding distances above the first row, and spawned in the same way. It will take three or four weeks before the spawn will have traveled over the entire bed, presenting the appearance of a fine gauze network through the manure, and sometimes visible on the surface. Five or six weeks from the time of making the bed small button Mushrooms will appear, if all the points have been carefully attended to. When the beds begin to bear the temperature of the cave, or building, should be kept steady at fifty-five degrees. A small amount of water is needed; it may be supplied occasionally with a watering-pot having a fine rose. The water used should be a few degrees above the cave, say sixty to sixty-three degrees.

A bed prepared in the way described will produce Mushrooms for six months. At the end of this time the beds should be renewed, and a steady supply can be had through the whole year. It is not absolutely necessary that the beds should be the shape named. If circumstances do not admit of it they may be made wider, but not less than two feet in thickness. As stated before, the important point is the careful preparation of the manure.

GATHERING.—In gathering the left hand should be placed on the bed along side of the Mushroom, then with the right hand it is turned and pulled at the same time. In this way less injury is done to the running spawn, and the bed will produce more than if the Mushrooms are jerked out without this precaution.

In our caves the yield was one quart to every ten feet daily. These sold readily at from seventy-five cents to one dollar per quart. Even at lower figures Mushrooms would pay a handsome profit.

Light should be excluded from the caves at all times, but ventilation must be had by means of valves on top. Candles or lamps should be used to give light for working.

Whatever method may be adopted for growing Mushrooms—and there are many in common practice—constant attention is required at all times to be successful in this branch of gardening.

## NASTURTIUM, OR INDIAN CRESS.

### *Tropæolum majus.*

The Nasturtium is a hardy annual, a native of Peru. It is grown in gardens as an ornamental plant, while at the same time the leaves and flowers are used for salads and garnishing. The seed-vessels, or berries, when gathered young, on a dry day, and put into vinegar, make a pickle, preferred by many persons to Capers.

The Nasturtium-seed should be planted two inches deep, in rows, along side of a trellis, or other support, in April or the beginning of May. An ounce of seed will be enough for twenty-five or thirty feet of row.

For covering trellis-work, unsightly fences, &c., &c., the "tall" variety should be sown; for forming borders the "dwarf" Nasturtium is the best. Sometimes the latter requires staking.

Although an annual when grown in the open air, the Nasturtium is a perennial when grown in the green-house.

## CHAPTER IX.
### ONION.

*Allium cepa.*

The Onion is well known, and highly prized as a garden vegetable, and, as a field-crop, is extensively cultivated in many sections of the country.

Wethersfield, Conn., Narraganset Shores, R. I., and Chester Meadows, New York, are a few of the districts where large tracts of land are annually devoted to the cultivation of the Onion.

It is also grown largely by market-gardeners, and is one of the most profitable crops, when the "sets" are planted on rich ground.

There is also a large and lucrative business carried on near Philadelphia in growing Onion "sets" for market. There is usually a good demand for them at prices ranging from five to ten dollars per bushel in the Spring of the year.

These three different branches of the Onion business need, to some extent, different methods of culture. It will be necessary, therefore, to treat them separately.

When grown as a field-crop, the land should be level, comparatively free from stones, or other obstructions, deep and mellow. The Onion will grow best on such a soil when well drained, either naturally or by artificial means. Fall ploughing, throwing the land into twelve-feet ridges is advisable. In the Spring an application of twenty to thirty two-horse loads of well-rotted yard or hog-pen manure, are spread broadcast and ploughed under. The ground is then ploughed, harrowed, and sometimes levelled with a wooden roller before sowing the seed. An application of two or three hundred pounds of ground bones to the acre will benefit the crop.

The seed is sown in drills, one foot apart, either for field or garden, by a machine, using four pounds of fresh seed to an acre. To insure the seed being well covered, a light roller is drawn by hand over the ground, in the direction of the rows. By marking the piece with the garden-marker and then sowing with Holbrook's seed-drill, there will be enough covering without any rolling.

The early running of the hand-hoes between the rows, is the only way to do in growing Onions for profit. If the weeds gain headway, the cultivation will cost ten times what it otherwise would. As soon as the rows are designated by the young plants, keep the scuffle and Onion-hoes active until the tops are large enough to give shade. Weeds appearing in the lines of the rows must be removed, before they attain any size, by hand—the boy carrying a knife with a curved point, made for the purpose. The seed sown early in April, the crop will be ready to harvest in the latter part of August or the beginning of September. The Onions are pulled out by hand, throwing three or four rows together and leaving them in this way for a few weeks, until they are dry enough to be stored—when they are gathered, carted and placed on a barn floor or loft until marketed. If kept over Winter, they should be protected by a covering of straw or salt hay, before cold weather sets in. Onions keep better with the tops left on, therefore they are not trimmed till a few days before sending them to market.

On land manured and well-worked, Onions will give a yield of five hundred bushels to the acre, and they will bring from fifty cents to seventy-five cents per bushel. For the last few years prices have averaged higher. They are worth four dollars a barrel, by the quantity, at present. As a rule, the Onion is grown on the same ground every year and it does better than by changing. It is important, therefore, to prevent any weeds from seeding.

In growing "set" Onions, the ground should be of a light character, not over rich, and thoroughly pulverized. The object is to get a large yield of very small Onions; the smaller the better, for if they grow much larger than a hickory nut, they are liable to run to seed instead of forming a bulb.

When the ground is made ready, early in April, by ploughing, harrowing, and levelling with rakes—a line is stretched, and the piece marked out with a garden-marker in rows nine inches or a foot apart. The seed is then put in by a seed-drill, using thirty-six to forty pounds of seed to an acre. The cultivation is all done with hand-tools in the same way as recommended above for growing Onions as a field-crop. No weeds should be permitted to grow either between or in the rows. On heavy ground, seed, when sown thickly, is liable to "damp off" before coming through the surface, and great losses are sometimes sustained from this cause. To make it more convenient for working, every eighth row is left blank; this will leave the young "sets" in narrow beds, turning the blank row into a walk.

These sets will be ripe in August; they are taken out of the ground and left on the rows to dry. They are then placed upon a loft, not more than eight or ten inches in thickness. They should be examined and turned occasionally, for if the weather is warm and damp, they may suffer some injury from rotting. When cold weather sets in, we put on a light covering of salt hay as a protection from the frost. A pound of seed when sown thickly, will give three or four bushels of "Set" Onions.

The market-gardener plants "sets" instead of sowing seed, on ground rich enough to produce early Cabbages, using from fifty to seventy two-horse loads of manure to the acre, turning it under and then making the surface level. The rows are marked out one foot apart, the "sets" distributed along each row three inches apart, and firmly pressed in place by hand, roots downward. This done, the earth is drawn over the rows by the feet. To give more ease in cultivating, every eighth row is left blank, for a passage-way.

The Onions soon start a vigorous growth, and the gardener is just as vigorous in his efforts to keep ahead of the weeds, by disturbing the whole surface before the weeds appear, and often enough to keep the ground loose and clean.

It will take from eight to ten bushels of "sets" to

plant an acre. One quart will be sufficient for the kitchen-garden.

The gardener usually sells his crop in the green state; it will be ready for market about the middle of June. The Onions are pulled, carried to the market-house, washed, and then bunched—in different sized bunches, if intended for different markets. For New York, from six to eight Onions are tied in one bunch; while for Newark, N. J., only three, and these bring from one dollar and fifty cents to two dollars per hundred bunches.

Onions, when grown in this way, are taken off in time to plant Celery or Spinach in the same ground. They will pay a profit of two to three hundred dollars an acre. They are a very sure crop, seldom failing when the ground is rich and the "sets" small at the time of planting. They can be grown from "sets" for Winter use, and kept the same as when produced from seed. Many of the most successful gardeners always select the best shaped Onion bulbs, to save for seed; by following this plan, there are no disappointments about seed not coming up well, and no getting a variety not true to name.

Seed Onions are kept through the Winter in the same way as recommended for market Onions.

Early in the Spring, the Onions for seed are set out in a piece of rich ground; two feet between the rows, two inches deep and six inches apart in the row. When the seed-stalks blossom, they sometimes need to be supported, to prevent them from falling over. The seed will be ripe in July, when the "heads" are cut off, placed on a tight floor, and when dry, thrashed out.

## 184 ONIONS.

INSECTS.—Occasionally, Onion growers suffer serious loss from the effects of the Onion Maggot (*Anthomyia ceparum*), a small fly that deposits an egg in the Onion near the ground. These eggs hatch in a short time, giving the maggot and then the change to the pupa state, from which comes the fly again. Dusting with fresh wood-ashes is said by many growers to be a preventive; or burning the surface over with old straw before sowing the seed,

EARLY RED.

and scattering powdered charcoal with a dressing of five bushels of salt to the acre.

Although we have grown Onions in a large way for many years, the maggot has never made its appearance with us. I am inclined to think the insect is a near relation of the *Anthomyia brassicæ*, and that dusting the plants with fresh air-slacked lime would be found of service; or sowing some fine flour of bone in the rows, still better.

VARIETIES.—There is a long list of varieties, but

## ONIONS. 185

practical Onion-growers confine themselves to a few kinds for their main crop.

EARLY RED.—A medium-sized Onion, very early, lighter in color than the Large Red, close flesh and a good keeper.

WETHERSFIELD LARGE RED is grown as a field-crop, extensively in the Eastern States, especially in Connecticut. It attains a large size—color dark red, rounding in shape, and has good keeping qualities.

WETHERSFIELD LARGE RED.

YELLOW DANVERS is a good variety for market-gardeners to grow from "sets," being superior in many respects to the kind commonly grown in that way, and known as the Yellow Dutch. It is straw-color, flesh close, and keeps as well in Winter as any other variety, besides being more productive than the Dutch.

ONIONS.

YELLOW DANVERS.

WHITE PORTUGAL.—This is a very mild and pleasantly flavored white variety, and on this account is grown generally for home use. It is more tender

WHITE PORTUGAL.

than the others named, and it does not keep as well during the Winter.

POTATO ONION is a popular variety for early

OKRA, OR GUMBO. 187

Spring planting in private gardens. It increases from the single bulb planted, forming a number of small ones. When set out in the Spring, in rows one foot apart and three inches apart in the row, they give a supply for table use early in the season. For the quantity of Onion-seed to sow in the kitchen-garden, see " List of Seeds for the Garden."

## OKRA, OR GUMBO.
*Hibiscus esculentus.*

The Okra is a native of the West Indies, where it has long been used for making Gumbo soup.

It is grown to some extent in private gardens in

OKRA.

the Northern States, but it is more generally cultivated farther south. The seed-pods, when green, are used in stews, soups, &c., &c. For this purpose, they should be gathered while young and tender; for when the pods grow older and harder, they are tough and tasteless.

We have been successful in growing the "dwarf" Okra in New Jersey, and we consider it the best variety to plant.

The seed should be sown in May, in rows two and a half feet between and one foot apart in the row. When the plants are well above the ground, hoe carefully, drawing the earth towards the plants, as with Lima Beans. Okra will do best in mellow, rich ground. The pods can be kept for Winter use, by slicing them and tying them up like dried apples. One ounce will be enough for family use.

## CHAPTER X

PARSLEY.

*Apium petroselinum.*

THE garden Parsley, a native of Sardinia, is a hardy biennial and is in general use in this country for garnishing, flavoring soups, stews, &c., &c. The peculiar smell of Parsley will neutralize the odor given to the breath by eating Onions.

It is grown to a limited extent by market-gardeners, either in frames or in the open ground, and when there is a demand, it pays a handsome profit—but as the demand is uncertain, gardeners seldom give a large space to its culture.

Parsley will do best in a deep, rich loam, thoroughly pulverized before sowing the seed. This should be done in April, in drills one foot apart, strewing the seed thickly, and covering by raking the surface with wooden rakes in the lines of the rows. The seed is slow to germinate, requiring two or three weeks before sprouting. A few Radish-seeds, sown in the rows at the time of sowing the Parsley-seed, will mark the lines so that a scuffle-hoe can be run through before the weeds start. Later in the season, the tops give an abundance of shade, and the weeds can be kept under with but little trouble. The tops are cut off in June, and again in August or September, when a new growth will start up. During November the Parsley is dug. It is sometimes "heeled in" in frames, under glass, thickly; or it is stowed away in trenches like Celery. A still more rapid and equally good method is to "pit" it in the way described for Horse-Radish, raising the pit only two feet high and keeping the tops on the outside.

DWARF CURLED PARSLEY.

When sown in frames, the seed is put in during the early part of April in rows between the Lettuce, running from front to rear. The tops will be ready for cutting in June, when they are tied in small bundles and sent to market. They are cut again later in the season, in September, and then the crop is dug up and stored before cold weather sets in.

One ounce of fresh seed will be enough for home use. This will sow about one hundred feet of row. When sown in frames, it will pay about two dollars per sash and to the extent that it can be grown in the open ground, from eight hundred dollars to one thousand dollars an acre. Last Winter one of my neighbors sold one hundred dollars' worth from the twelfth of an acre.

In preparing Parsley for market, it is washed and then tied in bunches, four or five stalks in each,

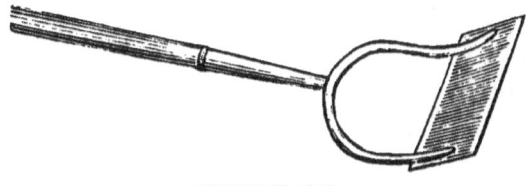

SCUFFLE-HOE.

leaving all the roots on. The DWARF CURLED is the best kind for the garden.

A few of the best specimens should always be kept to grow seed from the following season. Fresh seed should invariably be used, as old seed is not to be relied on.

HAMBURG PARSLEY.—This variety is plain-leaved, with more vigorous habits than the Dwarf Curled; it is cultivated for the roots, which frequently grow on rich ground to the size of medium Parsnips. They are boiled and served in the same manner as Parsnips. The seeds should be sown in drills eighteen inches apart, and when the plants are two inches high, they must be thinned out to three inches apart in the row.

## PARSNIP.
*Pastinaca sativa.*

The culture of this valuable root is principally confined to the kitchen and market-gardens. It is seldom grown in this country as a farm-crop for feeding stock, although it is one of the best on the list for this purpose. On soil free from stones and in good heart, Parsnips will yield from six to eight hundred bushels to the acre, at no greater expense for cultivation than is required for a crop of Ruta Bagas, only they need the whole season for maturing. The roots are perfectly hardy; they can be left in the ground all winter, then dug and fed to cattle in the Spring. Or a portion of the crop can be taken out and pitted, for Winter use, the same as Carrots (which see).

When Parsnips are fed to milch cows, the quality of the milk is improved, the cream is much richer, and the butter of finer flavor. Young stock are fond of them, and they will be found superior to any other root for fattening both neat-cattle and hogs.

When fresh seed is sown, the plants, while growing, need less attention than Carrots, owing to the leaves being long and spreading, giving shade which checks to some extent the rapid growth of weeds.

SOIL.—The Parsnip will give the largest yield on a deep, rich, sandy or clay loam. For this crop, we plough the ground in ridges, in the Fall; apply from fifteen to twenty-five two-horse loads of well-rotted manure in the Spring and plough it under. For field-culture, the treatment is, in every part, similar to that described for Carrots, with the single exception, that the seed is sown in April, or as early in the Spring as the ground is dry enough to be worked.

A few Radish-seeds sown at the same time, will mark the lines, so that a cultivator can be run through before the weeds start. When the plants are two or three inches high, they should be thinned out by hand, leaving them three inches apart in the row. The cultivation we do with a mule and a Carrot-weeder, keeping the surface loose and free from weeds, with very small outlay.

We use four to five pounds of fresh seed to an acre, and sow it by machine. Parsnip seed more than one year old cannot be trusted; seed from the previous year should always be sown. On our farm, the average yield is from six hundred to eight hundred bushels to an acre, and they are usually worth fifty cents a bushel, in market, when trimmed and washed. At times, during the winter, when the supply has been short, we have sold at prices ranging from two dollars to four dollars per barrel, holding two and a half bushels.

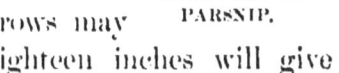
LONG SMOOTH PARSNIP.

In garden-culture, the rows may be left nearer together, eighteen inches will give enough space. Two ounces of seed will furnish an abundance for family use. Owing to the uncertainty of the seed germinating, it is better to sow thickly and thin out the young plants to three inches apart.

When digging the crop, in the Fall, careful gardeners select a few of the finest specimens, from which to grow seed the following year. These roots are transplanted into good ground in the Spring, and by July the seed will mature. In field-culture, when ready to harvest, by running a large-sized lifting sub-soil plough alongside of each row, the expense of getting out the crop will be lessened at least one half.

For many years we have grown the Long Smooth, or "Hollow Crowned," and consider it by far the best variety either for the kitchen-garden, market, or as a field-crop for cattle. When labor-saving implements are used, Parsnips can be grown at an expense not to exceed seventy dollars an acre.

PEA.

*Pisum sativum.*

The Pea is one of the favorite vegetables cultivated in the kitchen-garden as well as for market, in almost every section of this country. Green Peas, half-grown, when properly served, are a much-esteemed dish with most persons.

New Jersey and Long Island have long been noted for producing early Peas for the New York and Philadelphia markets, and on the kinds of soil where they were grown, they were a profitable farm crop. Of late years, since the close of the war, a large share of this business has been transferred from its original quarters to Virginia and South Carolina, where it is now carried on extensively by Southern gardeners, who ship the whole of their crop to Northern markets. These southern-grown Peas from Charleston reach New York in April and May, and they are closely followed by the crop from Norfolk, Va. These early arrivals have " cut " into the old business sadly, and have forced many growers in New Jersey to abandon Pea-growing, for profit.

The Pea flourishes best on light soil; it can be grown with less manure than most garden crops. In the vicinity of Charleston, S. C., fine crops of Early Peas have been produced on light, sandy soil, with an application, in the drill, of three hundred pounds of superphosphate of lime to the acre.

With better facilities for transportation from Charleston, the culture of the Pea could be made a profitable business, provided growers would realize the importance of careful picking and packing, which part of the work, so far, has been sadly neglected by many gardeners. " What is worth doing, is worth doing well." Of this, many shippers of Southern vegetables seem to be totally ignorant, and they reap the reward of low prices.

In the kitchen garden, Peas are usually " brushed " to keep the vines off the ground, but in field-culture the vines are permitted to fall down after the last ploughing, which throws a shallow furrow from either side, towards the rows of vines. In the field, the rows are marked out, with a one-horse plough, three feet apart, the manure applied in the furrow, then the seed distributed thinly, and covered by hand-hoes. The cultivation is done by horse tools, going through, may be, once with the hand-hoes to take out any weeds that may show themselves in the rows. One bushel and a quarter of seed is enough for an acre. The average return is from one hundred to one hundred and twenty-five bushels per acre, and gives a profit of from one hundred to one hundred and fifty dollars.

In garden-culture, to save time in "brushing," Peas are sown in double rows, that is, two rows are put in, only eight inches apart, and then a space of two feet is left for a passage-way—one line of brush will support the two rows.

For an early crop, they should be sown as soon as the ground can be worked. A slight frost does not injure the vines. We have frequently had young vines covered with snow, early in April, without suffering any harm.

To keep the table well supplied, a sowing should be made every two or three weeks, until the first of July.

When planted in April, the early or main crop will be ready for market or home use in July, in time to make a second planting.

Of course, the times of sowing will depend on the locality. In South Carolina, Peas are sown in December and January, while in New Jersey they are seldom planted before the first of April, and some seasons as late as the middle of the month. A few years ago my brothers shipped, from Charleston, Peas on the fourteenth of April, and they reached New York when we were sowing our early crop.

With Peas, the list of varieties is a long one—but there are a few well-known kinds that are general favorites.

PHILADELPHIA EXTRA EARLY is the best early variety that we have tested, both for garden and field-culture. It is more productive, of better quality, and several days earlier than the Daniel O'Rourke, when planted along side, and with the same treatment.

DANIEL O'ROURKE.—The vines of this kind will not average more than two feet high. It has been a favorite market variety, because all the pods fill out about the same time, enabling the gardener to gather the crop in two or three pickings.

TOM THUMB is grown in private gardens on account of its requiring no "brushing." The vines only grow about eight or ten inches high. The yield is large, but the Peas are of medium quality. We sow this kind late, and it does equally well as when sown early.

MCLEAN'S LITTLE GEM is in habits similar to the Tom Thumb, but in quality far superior.

BISHOP'S LONG POD is a favorite sort in many sections for family use. The pods are large and abundant. The vines are not inclined to grow very tall. It is a good variety to follow the early kinds.

CHAMPION OF ENGLAND, an old and well-known Pea, is without doubt the best late variety grown. The vines grow from three to four feet high, and require "brushing," to keep them from the ground.

BLACK AND WHITE MARROWFATS are also tall-growing sorts. They are still planted extensively for late market varieties, and for this purpose are highly esteemed.

BLUE IMPERIAL is a first quality, late variety, and has a delicate flavor when gathered before the Peas have grown full size. This remark can be applied to every variety of Pea cultivated.

A couple or three quarts of as many of the varieties, sown in succession, will keep the table abundantly supplied with this delicious vegetable.

## PEPPER.

### Capsicum.

The Pepper is cultivated to some extent in private gardens and quite extensively as a market crop, very frequently by contract for pickle factories. Although prices are generally low when contracted for, the yield is so large, when the crop does well, that a large profit is often realized from the sale of Peppers.

The seed should be sown in a hot-bed in March, giving the plants the same treatment as Egg Plants, with this exception, they need not be transplanted, but they may be left in the seed-bed until they are removed to the open ground in June.

There is little or no demand for Peppers in market until late in the Fall, so there is nothing gained by having them before October. They will grow best on a rich, moist loam, inclining to lightness, although they will yield bountifully on any well-prepared soil.

In the garden or field, they may be set out with the "dibble," in the same way as Cabbage plants, about the middle of June, leaving two feet between the rows, and the plants eighteen inches apart in the row. The ground should be kept loose and clean by frequent disturbances of the soil.

A dozen plants will be enough in a garden for family use. These can be bought from some gardener, near by, cheaper than they can be raised.

Unless for pickle factories, the demand in market is limited; but to the extent that they are wanted, it is profitable to grow them. They will usually sell from seventy-five cents to one dollar per hundred; this would be at the rate of four to five hundred dollars per acre.

VARIETIES.—There are only a few kinds grown in this country.

SWEET MOUNTAIN is of large size, similar in shape to the Bell, but milder. It is used for making mangoes.

BULL-NOSE, OR BELL, is large, slightly tapering, rather mild, and desirable for pickling. It matures early and bears abundantly.

SQUASH.—This variety is different in shape from the above. It is more and deeply ribbed, stronger to the taste than the other two, and used extensively for pickling.

CAYENNE.—This is a small variety, the fruit long and tapering, bright red when ripe, and very strong. It does, when ground furnish the pepper of commerce.

POTATO.

*Solanum tuberosum.*

From each successive year's experience, the shrewd farmer draws a practical lesson, which, if properly applied, will materially assist in making his special calling a success. There is very little to be made in farming or gardening by the game of chance, or, as it is sometimes called, "good luck," but industry well directed, will eventually be rewarded, while carelessness and mismanagement are just as certain to reap their reward.

Every branch of industry has, from various causes, to battle against a "blue" season, and farming or gardening forms no exception to the rule. At present, farm wages are high, with no indications of any change for the better. My neighbor asks, "How, under existing circumstances, are farmers to make ends meet?" My reply is, substitute horse for hand-labor, adopt better methods of culture, concentrate the work and manure on fewer acres, so as to produce maximum crops, and by these means lessen the cost per bushel of producing. The expense of cultivating is the same, whether the yield is one hundred or three hundred bushels of Potatoes to the acre.

The Potato crop is an important one in every State and Territory in this country. Two hundred bushels to the acre is not a large return from well-fertilized and properly tilled ground; still we find that the average crop of the country is not quite one hundred, even in favorable seasons. Taking the price of Potatoes at seventy-five cents per bushel, by adopting better methods of culture, the increased value in the United States of this crop alone would amount to over seventy-five millions of dollars a year.

Although the price of Potatoes has only advanced a trifle within the past ten years, and farm wages and other farm expenses have nearly doubled, yet I feel confident that I can make as much per acre now, cultivating Potatoes, as in 1860; simply by making use of the methods named, and planting varieties of Potatoes that are more productive than the Mercer or Prince Albert. There is no system of farming so perfect as not to be susceptible of improvement; and the intelligent farmer is always ready to make a change or follow a new method of culture, when it is evident that, by so doing, he will increase the product per acre or lessen the expense of producing.

Our method of cultivating Potatoes, which has given entire satisfaction for the last three years, is substantially as follows. The ground, which is a heavy clay, and naturally very poor, is Fall-ploughed, throwing it into " lands " about twenty feet wide, and left in this state until Spring. When the soil is dry enough to be worked, in April, it has a second ploughing, crosswise—never turning the soil less than ten inches deep. The manure is then spread broadcast on the surface, the quality of the soil regulating the quantity. However, we seldom use less than twenty two-horse loads of barn-yard manure or compost to each acre. When fish guano is used, it is mixed with soil for a week or two before planting-time, and then spread over the surface at the rate of from three-quarters to a ton to the acre. When barn-yard manure is used, the ground is harrowed before spreading the manure and with special fertilizers, such as phosphate, bone-dust, or guano; the harrowing is done after applying the manure, giving the ground only one "scrape," to level the surface. We change the seed every two years. For seed, I prefer large-sized Potatoes, cut into two, three, and four pieces, a fortnight at least before planting, and then dusted with wood-ashes. This I have done in wet or inclement weather during the month of March, when the men cannot work to advantage out of doors. With everything in readiness for planting, the seed Potatoes are put into barrels, carted to the field and placed at convenient distances across the lot, so that the persons "dropping" will lose no time and waste no strength in carrying the Potatoes from one end of the field to the other. This may appear trifling, but I find, when this plan is carried out, the work goes on more rapidly, and two persons will drop as much as three, when no system is practised. From the effects of the Fall ploughing, the alternate freezing and thawing during Winter, and with a ploughing in Spring, the ground will turn up kind and mellow, just in the right tilth for planting. The Potatoes are put in at the third ploughing, in the following manner. Commencing at one side of the field, twenty or thirty feet from the fence, the ploughman with his horses strikes a straight furrow and returns with a back furrow. On the second time around, the droppers follow the plough, placing the Potatoes from fifteen to eighteen inches apart in the loose ground just turned over, and in a position so that the next furrow-slice will cover the seed about four inches deep. The furrow-slices will average from ten to twelve inches in width, and the seed is planted in every third furrow on either side of the starting-point; this will leave the rows of Potatoes about three feet apart. This is wide enough to admit a horse-hoe for cultivating during the early stages of growth. By the system of back-furrowing there is no time wasted, either by the persons dropping or the man with the plough. We employ two German women, who drop as fast as the two horses will plough the ground and cover the Potatoes. On loose, mellow soil, this force will plant, on an average, two acres a day, working ten hours. In this way, the soil is left in better condition to facilitate the growth of the young Potatoes than by any of the methods in general use, that I have heretofore practised in growing Potatoes for market. The seed is placed in the side of the furrow-slice, and is not displaced by the horse that walks in the furrow. Occasionally the plough is thrown out by the point striking a stone, and one or two of the seed left without covering, but in the next time around, this can be repaired and the seed properly covered.

With a very little practice, the ploughman will run each furrow as straight as a "bee-line." I never have had rows of Potatoes come up more evenly than for the past three years, when planted in this way.

Another method is, when the ground is ready to open the furrow with a one-horse plough, spreading the manure in the furrow; then the Potatoes are dropped in place along the bottom of the furrow, and, by means of the plough again, are covered about three inches deep. When the young stocks are just coming through the surface, the field is harrowed, running the harrow in the line of the rows. We use for this purpose a blunt-toothed harrow, which levels the surface, destroys the first crop of young weeds, and as far as I am capable of observing, does no injury to the Potatoes. I am aware that many Potato-growers condemn the harrow for this purpose, as doing more harm than good. When I am convinced that this is the fact, I will at once abandon its use and adopt some other improved implement to do the same kind of work.

When the young plants are well above the surface, I run Howe's horse-hoe or Perry's Scarifier between the rows, going twice in each space, and as close to the stocks as it is possible, without cutting them. This operation is repeated once at least every two weeks, until the Potatoes come into blossom, when the cultivation is stopped. Sometimes a few heavy showers of rain will compact and harden the surface; in such a case, we use Mapes' one-horse lifting sub-soil plough to run once in the middle, between the rows, and loosen the soil three or four inches deep. Our plan is to prepare the soil thoroughly before planting, and then, during the growing season, to keep merely two or three inches of the surface loose and free. There is little or no hard labor required by following this system of culture. In an ordinary season, the horse-tools will do all the work necessary to keep the surface loose and free from weeds. I make it a rule, however, to go through the field once with the hand-hoes, cutting out any weeds that may be growing in the .nes of the rows where the horse-tools cannot reach. Under good management, Potatoes should be kept free from weeds and grass, until they are in full blossom. After this date, cultivation may be suspended, for any weeds that may then come up, do little or no injury to the crop. The stalks shade the ground so that the growth of weeds is sparse; although it is often advisable to have some scattering tall weeds pulled by hand, before the Potatoes are dug.

In cultivating early varieties of Potatoes on strong ground, they can be harvested in time to get a crop of Turnips off the same ground, which may prove as profitable as the crop of Potatoes.

We grow on our farm from one thousand to one thousand five hundred bushels of Potatoes a year for market. During the past ten years we have sold none less than seventy-five cents per bushel, by the quantity, and a large proportion of them would average one dollar a bushel.

On ground well manured and tilled, two hundred bushels of marketable Potatoes to the acre is about an average crop in our section; these are worth one hundred and seventy-five dollars. Deducting the expense, there is left from one hundred to one hundred and twenty-five dollars. With early Potatoes, harvested in time to sow a Fall crop of Yellow Stone Turnips, which often yield as much as the Potatoes, there will be a net from both crops of about two hundred dollars an acre. Last Summer we dug from an acre of Early Rose, one hundred and ten barrels, and sold them at three dollars and twenty-five cents per barrel, for table use.

HARVESTING.—Although we have tested numerous Potato-digging machines, there is none that has given us satisfaction. We still hold to the old method of removing the stalks, then, with a plough, throwing a furrow away from either side of the row, and turning out the Potatoes with the digging-fork. By this method a man can easily get out thirty bushels a day, at an expense of from five to six cents a bushel.

STORING POTATOES.—Potatoes for table use should be stored in a cool, dry, dark cellar. They will keep better if a small quantity of soil is mixed in with them at the time of putting them away. When Potatoes are left exposed to the sunlight, they soon turn green, a bitter principle is evolved, and when cooked, they have a nauseating and unpleasant taste. Every observing farmer knows that it often happens, either from the washing away of the earth, or from careless hoeing, that a portion of the Potatoes in a "hill" is left exposed to the light. These Potatoes soon change color, and are worthless for table use. This kind of exposure also hastens decay, no matter where the Potatoes are kept. Even when purchased for family use, in small quantities, say a barrel or a bushel at a time, they should be kept in a dark corner of the cellar.

POTATOES. 207

VARIETIES.—There is a long catalogue of varieties of Potatoes, many of which have only a local reputation. The old favorite Mercer is no longer

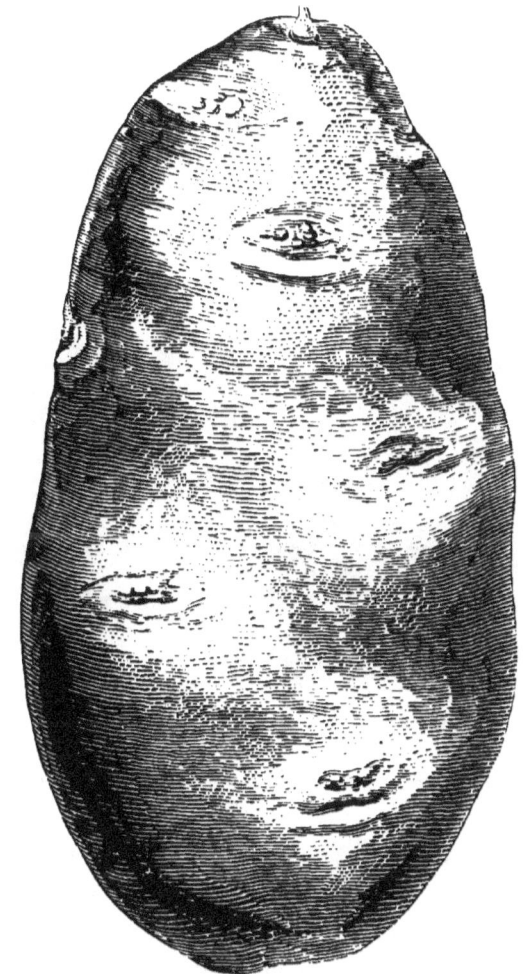

EARLY ROSE.

cultivated to any extent. The Carter, too, has passed away, with twenty other kinds that once were popular. The seedlings of the late Professor Goodrich are quietly dropped from the approved lists for general culture, and their places filled by other and more promising sorts. How long these varieties will hold their place in public estimation experience only can tell.

We give six illustrations of Potatoes, the representative sorts for the different seasons, and good types of their kinds.

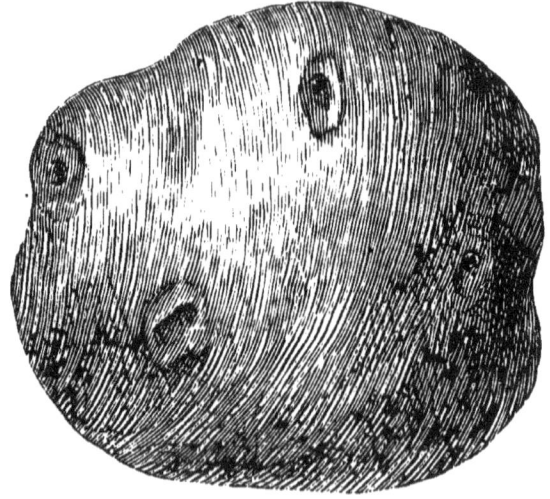

DYKEMAN.

Among the most popular early varieties may be named the

EARLY ROSE, a seedling introduced by Mr. Breese, of Vermont. With three years' trial it has attained a national reputation. It is well worthy of it, for it is the best early variety that we have at present, either for family use or for market.

The Rose is a large-sized Potato, smooth skin, few eyes, flesh white, and steams or boils mealy.

POTATOES. 209

DYKEMAN is an old standard, cultivated by Long Island gardeners extensively for the New York market.

PEERLESS.

PEERLESS is more productive and larger than the Early Rose, equal to it in quality, and is, for a late variety, what the Rose is for the early.

210                POTATOES.

Peach Blow has always been a favorite, and a standard of excellence in quality. It is a large, round potato, takes the whole season to mature, and is difficult to boil evenly on account of its shape. It is also subject to the rot.

PEACH BLOW.

Gleason is a seedling of the Garnet-Chili. It grows large, roundish, and has a peculiar roughness of skin, by which it can always be distinguished. It is a late variety and of good quality.

Kidney.—Medium size, productive, of fine qual

ity for home use. It keeps well, retaining its good quality through the Winter.

Jackson White is cultivated extensively, as a late variety, for market. It is long, the eyes deeply set, quality good when grown on dry ground.

GLEASON.

Early Mohawk is an early variety, recently introduced, very productive, but inferior in quality— about equal to the Harrison for cooking.

Insects.—The Potato is liable to the attacks of various insects, both in the foliage as well as the tubers. For a number of years past the English wire-worm has seriously injured the Potatoes in New Jersey. The grub feeds upon the young tubers, dis-

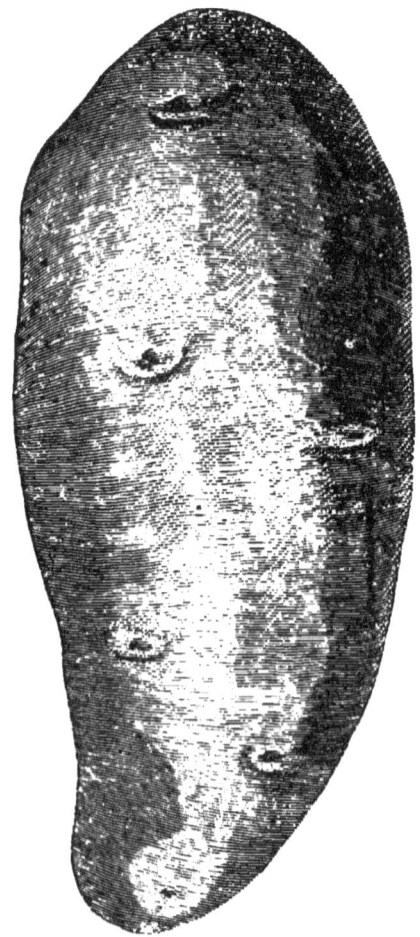

KIDNEY.

figuring them so much as to make them unsalable. The grub of the *Elaters*, that injures the Potato, is long and slender, having a hard, smooth skin, of a brownish yellow color, and, according to Harris, lives in its feeding state five years.

An application of ashes has been recommended as a remedy; but we have not found it to be of any service. Rape cake, broken into small pieces and scattered in different places through the field, attracts

COLORADO POTATO BUG.

the grubs; they collect to feed upon it, and large numbers may be destroyed.

The Colorado Potato bug (*Doryphora decemlineata*), has been doing mischief in the West, but it has not reached New Jersey or any of the Eastern States. These bugs appear in great numbers, destroying all the foliage and injuring the crop very seriously. Dusting with powdered White Hellebore is said to check them. A. D. Compton recommends a solution, made of one part salt, ten of soap, and twenty of water, for syringing the vines and effectually checking the bugs.

A correspondent of the Farmers' Club recommends one part of Paris green and twenty parts of flour of bone, mixed and sifted on the vines, an excellent remedy. One pound of the green will be enough for an acre.

The directions given for the field management of Potatoes can easily be adopted in garden-culture.

One bushel of seed will yield about twenty bushels of Potatoes, if planted on good ground and well tended.

## JERUSALEM ARTICHOKE.

*Helianthus tuberosus.*

The Jerusalem Artichoke, or the tuber-bearing Sunflower, as it is sometimes called, is a hardy perennial, a native of Brazil, the roots of which, in this country, are principally used for pickling.

When once this plant takes possession in the garden or field, it is almost impossible to eradicate it. It continues to grow from year to year in the same spot; no matter with what care the tubers have been taken out, there will be enough left to produce a crop the following year.

On this account it is an unpopular plant for garden-culture, for in a few years it would over-run everything else.

It will grow on very poor soil, and could with

advantage be planted in waste ground; along the fences (instead of briars); in the orchard; and in the Fall the pigs will feed and thrive upon the tuber. Even on thin light soil the Jerusalem Artichoke will yield from two hundred to three hundred bushels to the acre, and can be grown with profit, for feeding hogs and cattle. The tubers are not injured by freezing, and are quite as nutritive as the Potato. It is propagated by planting, in rows two and a half feet apart, and two feet in the row, medium-sized tubers, and covering them with three or four inches of soil.

In the Fall, the tubers that are wanted for Winter use may be dug up and kept during the Winter in a cellar, covered with sand.

Two quarts of tubers planted in some convenient spot outside of the garden, will give enough for family use.

## PUMPKIN.

### *Cucurbita pepo.*

There are innumerable variety of Pumpkins, but only a few of them are worthy of cultivation. None of them should ever be planted in the garden. By the travel of the *farina fecunda* of the Pumpkin, Melons, Cucumbers and Squashes will be hybridized and spoiled after the first year.

The Pumpkin rightly belongs in the field, and under good care bears abundantly, and furnishes a large amount of palatable food for cows, pigs, &c., &c.

They are used more extensively for pies. Grocers usually lay in a large stock of the Cheese Pumpkin in the Fall, to supply their customers with Country Pumpkins during the Winter.

They may be grown on waste land when manured in the hill (for they are rank feeders), planted eight feet apart each way any time in May. They are generally planted among Corn. The Cheese Pumpkin is the best for this purpose.

## CHAPTER XI.

RADISHES.

*Rhaphanus sativus.*

THE Radish is a general favorite with all classes. It is found in all well-managed private gardens, and early in the Spring it is grown extensively by market-gardeners in the vicinity of large cities. For the first Radishes that reach market, the seed is sown in hot-beds in January or February, and they are ready for use early in March. Gardeners who have put up "forcing-houses" within the last two years near New York, devote a portion of the tables to forcing Radishes, and find them to be as profitable, to the extent of the demand, as Lettuce. They give a profit of about one dollar and twenty-five cents a sash, 3 x 6, for each crop, and occupy the space only six or seven weeks, while it takes nine weeks for a crop of Lettuce.

Early Radishes are shipped from Norfolk to New York; they usually bring high prices—four to six dollars per hundred bunches, or from eight to ten dollars per barrel.

The Radish, like most of the vegetables, will grow best on a deep, rich, sandy loam. It must have a rapid growth to be of fine quality.

There are several methods practised by gardeners in growing Radishes. We always sow the seed thinly in the rows with early Beets and Carrots. The Radishes are pulled and sold before the Beets or Carrots need the room, and at the same time it gives us a chance to cultivate these crops earlier than we otherwise could. This plan can be just as well followed in the private garden; and by sowing a few Radish-seeds in the rows with each "row-crop" planted, the table can be kept supplied with young Radishes during the season.

On Long Island, they frequently devote the whole field to Radishes, sowing the seed broadcast and harrowing it in, or in rows one foot apart, using about five pounds of seed to the acre. This crop is taken off in full time to prepare the ground for a crop of late Cabbages.

Of late years, the profits from growing Radishes have not been large. It is considerable trouble to prepare them for market, especially the long Scarlet, making the flat bunches, washing, &c., &c. With a good crop, Radishes seldom pay more than one hundred to one hundred and fifty dollars an acre. We have known many and many an acre that did not yield fifty dollars.

When they first come into market from the open ground, near New York, they bring two dollars per hundred bunches; they fall very soon, as the supply increases, to one dollar or fifty cents a hundred, and are often dull at these prices.

The Radish is frequently retarded, and, in fact, the crop destroyed by a grub, *Anthomyia raphani*. This little insect deposits an egg in the root of the

Radish just under the surface, and in a short time appears the maggot, which feeds upon the young Radish. The best remedy that we know for this destructive insect is to apply a dressing of common salt (half a bushel on a rod of ground) to the surface in the Fall, and in the Spring when the ground is ready for planting, give a top-dressing of fresh air-slacked lime—or sprinkle some in the row, before sowing the seed—or in addition to the top-dressing of lime, apply fine bone-meal in the drill with the seed. I have tested the salt and bone, and always with good results, even on ground where, previous to this treatment, Radishes could not be grown.

There are only a few varieties of Radishes that are grown to any extent, either in the kitchen-garden or for market.

EARLY SCARLET TURNIP grows rapidly, medium size, shape round, when young delicate in flavor and very popular.

EARLY SCARLET TURNIP.

EARLY SHORT-TOP LONG SCARLET is well known as the standard variety, both for home use and the early Spring crop for market. When cultivated on a rich, sandy loam, the roots are long, smooth, and the quality first-rate while young.

WHITE SPANISH is a Summer variety, popular among Germans for making salads, and cultivated to some extent for that purpose. It is oblong, similar in shape to the Black Spanish, strong and biting, and seldom used by Americans.

## RADISHES.

BLACK SPANISH is a black Radish of large size, grown for Winter use. The seed should be sown in

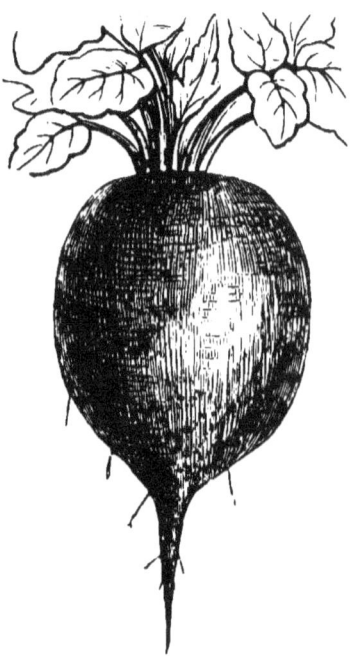

BLACK SPANISH.

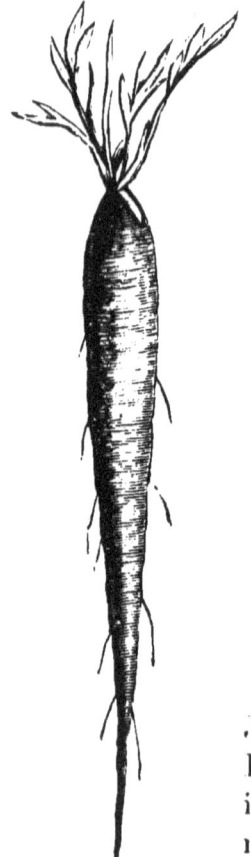

EARLY SHORT-TOP LONG SCARLET.

July, and the roots pitted in the Fall, like Turnips or Carrots. It is used principally by the Germans and French.

OLIVE-SHAPED is a small variety, oblong, color similar to the early Scarlet, of good quality and a favorite for home use.

Four ounces of seed, of the different varieties named, sown at different times, will keep the table well supplied with young Radishes.

## RHUBARB.

*Rheum hybridum.*

The Rhubarb is a hardy perennial, cultivated in this country exclusively for the leaf-stocks. There is a large demand for it during April, May and June for making pies, tarts, &c., &c. It sells well until green gooseberries, currants, and early apples come into market, when its season is over.

To show how the demand for Rhubarb has increased—fifteen years ago, with all our efforts, we could, on a regular market-day in Newark, dispose of no more than one hundred and fifty bunches. Now, we often put one thousand bunches on the wagon at one time, and, in the same market, find less trouble to sell them than we did the smaller number at first.

When grown for market, the profit depends on the earliness. This is obtained by planting in a favorable locality and heavy manuring. We usually send the first Rhubarb to market from the open ground about the twenty-fifth of April. It is always tied in bunches of from five to eight stocks of the early sorts, and from three to five of the later ones. At first, it sells freely at from fourteen dollars to sixteen dollars per hundred bunches; as the season advances the supply increases, and the prices fall gradually to six dollars or four dollars per hundred.

Our bed has been producing for the last seventeen years; it has paid at the rate of from three hundred dollars to five hundred dollars an acre. When once planted, Rhubarb gives less trouble than any other vegetable. We give our patch a heavy dressing of manure every Spring, and fork it under; two hoeings through the season will keep down the weeds. The cost of keeping an acre in good order will average about sixty dollars a year. Before planting, the ground should be ploughed and sub-soiled thoroughly, and, if necessary, drained. Then plenty of well-rotted manure should be turned under—sixty to seventy two-horse loads to the acre: the greater the quantity of manure used, the larger and finer will the Rhubarb grow.

The roots should be set four feet apart each way, using a spade and line, so as to make the rows straight and at regular distances. The plants should be divisions of old roots of the different kinds wanted. Cahoon's Seedling is the only kind that we know that will produce itself from seeds; the other well-known sorts will give a dozen varieties, and therefore they cannot be relied upon.

It makes little or no difference whether the roots are set out in the Spring or Fall—the condition of the ground is more important than the time of planting. It is well, however, when the roots have been in place for eight or nine years to take them up and divide them; this can be done in August. If the roots are carefully separated, part of a crop can be gathered the following year, and a full one the second year.

By placing a bottomless barrel over a crown in March, and putting some long manure on the outside, Rhubarb can be brought forward. Gardeners often force it by placing the roots under the tables in green and forcing-houses, or by means of an ordinary hot-bed. Prices are high and the demand good for this early Rhubarb, and it pays very well for the trouble. Twelve roots planted in rich soil in the garden will give an abundance for family use.

There are only a few varieties cultivated to any extent in this country.

MYATT'S LINNÆUS is the best early variety. It is grown extensively in private gardens and for the early crop for market. It is the best flavored kind with which we are familiar.

VICTORIA is later, but it has a much larger and longer leaf-stock than the Linnaeus, and on this account it is cultivated by gardeners for the main crop late in the season.

CAHOON'S SEEDLING is also a late variety. It grows even a larger stock than the Victoria, but it is stringy when the leaf-stocks attain full size, though very juicy.

This is the kind that has been sold by unprincipled men as the "Wine Plant"—one of the most flagrant swindles ever practised on the farming and gardening community.

## CHAPTER XII.

### SALSIFY, OR VEGETABLE OYSTER.

*Tragopogon porrifolius.*

The Salsify is a hardy biennial. It is cultivated for its roots, which seldom grow larger than small-sized Carrots or Parsnips.

It will succeed best on a deep, sandy loam, and treated in every way like Carrots. The seeds, which resemble an inferior quality of Oats, should be sown in drills, in April, and thinned out to two inches apart when the plants are well above ground. The roots are hardy; they may be left in the ground during the Winter, without injury. As they are used for culinary purposes during the Winter and early Spring, we dig them up in the Fall, and store them in trenches, like Celery, where they keep in good condition until wanted.

Salsify is grown to a limited extent for market. In preparing it for this purpose the fibrous roots and dead leaves are removed; it is then washed and tied in bunches about the size of Asparagus bunches. They usually bring one dollar and fifty cents a dozen bunches.

The Salsify is a favorite in the kitchen-garden, and it is becoming more so every year. It is easily grown.

Two ounces of seed will be sufficient for home use.

Some of the plants may be left in the ground all Winter for the seed. Rabbits are fond of the young tops in the Spring; we have frequently been annoyed by their eating the tops so closely that we have not been able to get any seed the second season.

### SCORZONERA.

*Scorzonera hispanica.*

The Scorzonera is a native of Spain. It is very similar to Salsify, and needs the same kind of culture. The seed should be sown early in April, as it requires a long season to mature.

It is used in soups, or boiled, and served as Salsify, it makes a pleasant dish. Before cooking, the outside skin should be taken off.

### SEA KALE.

*Crambe maritima.*

The Sea Kale is a hardy perennial, a native of the sea coast of Europe, where it grows abundantly. In its wild state, when blanched, gathered, and served as Asparagus, it is a delicious vegetable. Although extensively cultivated and very popular in Europe, it is grown to a very limited extent in this country in private gardens.

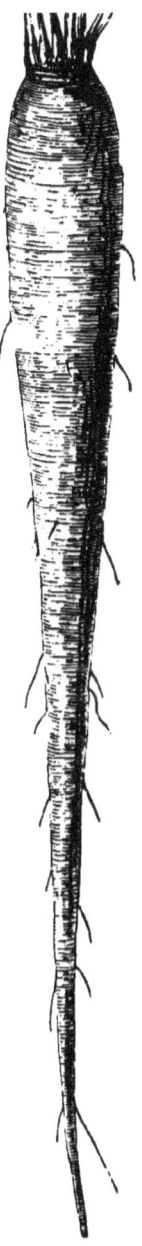

SALSIFY.

It may be propagated from roots or seeds, and it does best when planted on a deep, sandy loam. The least expensive way to start a bed, is to sow the seed in hills, two feet apart each way, early in April, and when the plants come up, thin out leaving only two to each place. Before sowing the seed, however, the bed should be thoroughly prepared, for on this will depend the success of the crop. The ground should be hoed frequently the first year, and no weeds allowed to appear. In the Fall, a mulch of long manure, three or four inches in thickness, should be put on the bed to protect against the cold weather.

Two ounces of seed will furnish enough plants for family use.

When propagated by roots, a few old ones may be lifted in the Fall, divided and kept buried in damp sand until the following Spring, when they may be set in place, covering the "crowns" four inches. Or the roots can be started in hot-beds in March and transplanted in place in April.

With this treatment, stocks for table use can be cut the first season. In the Spring of the second year, the bed should be forked over, turning in some of the mulch. The lighter part of it should be gathered in heaps, mixed with some leaf-mold, and, before the plants start to grow, placed on the "crowns," to blanch them. This Spring mulch should be eight or ten inches in thickness.

Large flower-pots covering the "crowns" will answer the same purpose, the object being to exclude the light. A slight dressing of common salt, every Spring, will be found beneficial. All the cutting of the Sea Kale is made at one time; while young the cutting should not be too close, for it would weaken the roots. When the flower heads appear, the mulch should be removed, and then the growth is not unlike that of Broccoli; it can be used in the same way. Sea Kale, served the same as Asparagus, is by many persons preferred to it.

### SPINACH.

*Spinacea oleracea.*

The Spinach is well and favorably known in every section of this country. It is cultivated very generally for Winter and Spring "greens" in all well-managed kitchen-gardens, and it is also a profitable crop for market.

It needs a deep, rich soil to produce maximum crops, for it can only be grown with profit on land that is well drained and highly manured. For a succession, the seed may be sown early in April and again in May—for the principal crop, from the first to the tenth of September, on ground from which a Summer crop has been taken.

Before sowing, the ground should be well-manured, thoroughly pulverized, and the surface levelled. The rows are then marked out, one foot apart, with the garden "marker." The seed can be sown in the garden by hand, and in the field with a machine, using five or six pounds to the acre. A quarter of a pound of seed will sow enough for home use.

During October, it is well to give the Spinach a hoeing, and thin it out in places where it is too thick.

What is wanted for home use in mid-Winter should be mulched lightly with salt hay; this will protect the leaves from injury by frost. Or if the Spinach has grown full size in the Fall, it may be kept very well by cutting it then, placing it three or four inches thick in a frame, and covering it with a sash and a little rubbish. Gardeners sometimes get eight and ten dollars a barrel in mid-Winter for Spinach kept in this way.

The main crop is cut and marketed during April and May, at prices ranging from one to five dollars per barrel, according to the supply, &c. When the ground is rich and the seed fresh, one hundred barrels to the acre is a large yield; although we have cut a barrel of Spinach from a square rod of ground.

When the Spinach is taken off, Tomatoes, Egg Plants, or Cabbages can be planted on the same ground. With a favorable season, an acre of Spinach will give from one hundred and fifty to two hundred dollars profit.

The varieties cultivated are but few in number.

Round Spinach is the most popular kind for home use or market. The seed is smooth, the leaves large and slightly crimped. It will stand the Winter without protection.

Prickly, or Fall.—This variety is said to be more hardy than the Round, but we have never found it to be so. Although recommended for Fall planting, it will grow just as well when sown in the Spring. The Prickly is not quite as productive as the Round Leaf, but fully equals it in quality.

## NEW ZEALAND SPINACH.

*Tetragonia expansa.*

This plant is a native of New Zealand, and in its habits is directly the opposite of the common Spinach. It stands the heat better than the cold; when the seeds are sown in a bed in April and transplanted in rows in May—three feet apart, and two feet apart in the row—it will give an abundance of greens during hot weather. These are cooked and served in the same manner as Spinach.

## SHALLOTS.

*Allium ascalonicum.*

The Shallot, sometimes called "Scallion," has a stronger taste than the Onion, but it does not leave the peculiar odor in the breath that the Onion does. It is used in this country, early in Spring, in its green state, to flavor soups, stews, &c., &c. It is generally found in private gardens and is also grown by market-gardeners as a source of profit.

The "sets" are planted in September, in rich ground, in rows, one foot apart, and three or four inches apart in the row. The smallest "sets" are the best for this purpose; they do not mould, and they are seldom injured by frost. These are ready for use in April; if not pulled then, they may be left in the ground until ripe. This is indicated by the leaves dying. By this time the bulbs will have increased in size very much, and they can easily be divided for planting again in the Fall.

A quart of these "offsets" will be enough for family use.

## SORREL.

*Rumex acetosa.*

The Sorrel is a perennial —seldom cultivated by American gardeners.

It is a popular vegetable with the French, who use it in various ways—for making salads, flavoring soups and stews, and sometimes they serve it plain as Spinach.

We have tried several times to eat Sorrel, served in French style, but we had to give it up. It is said to be a very healthful vegetable.

Sorrel is very easily cultivated. The seed may be sown in drills one foot apart, in April, and in ninety days there will be an abundant crop of large, succulent leaves.

## SQUASH.

*Cucurbita Species.*

The Squash is extensively cultivated in the kitchen-garden and also as a profitable market crop. There is a long list of varieties, all of them of tropical origin, and consequently tender. As the young plants are so sensitive to cold, we seldom put in the seed before the middle of May, when the ground is warm and the weather settled. The Squash will do well on any properly prepared soil, but a sandy loam is better adapted to this vegetable than soil of a heavier character.

For the Early Bush sorts we make hills the same as for Cucumbers and Melons, four feet between the rows and three feet in the rows, using about the same quantity of well-rotted manure. Six or eight seeds are planted in each hill. When three rough leaves are formed, all but three plants to a hill should be pulled out.

As the young plants are liable to the attacks of the "*Striped Bug*," the remedy recommended for Cucumbers should be applied to the Squash vines.

The later varieties are cultivated in the same manner, only making the hills eight feet apart each way. The space between the hills can be planted with Lettuce, or Kohl-Rabi, for an early crop, where economy of ground is essential. No weeds should be allowed to appear among the vines.

On Long Island and in some parts of New Jersey the early kinds are grown as field-crops; but the sale of them is very uncertain. We have seen growers who, one year, were forced to consign a large part of their crop to the hog-pen; the next season the same space devoted to Squash gave a profit of one hundred and twenty-five dollars.

The Early Bush varieties are grown largely around Norfolk and Charleston, but even when brought from so far South, the profits are not high, seldom being more than one hundred and twenty-five dollars an acre. When the expenses are deducted from this amount, the profit is still less.

The varieties of Squash are numerous, but those generally grown are but few.

EARLY WHITE BUSH is one of the earliest and best kinds for market or home use.

EARLY YELLOW BUSH.—Similar to the above, only differing in color. Plant four by three.

## SQUASH.

EARLY BUSH SUMMER CROOKNECK is an old favorite variety for summer use. The vines are compact and bear abundantly. The fruit is yellow, covered thickly with warty excrescences, and grows eight or nine inches long. Plant four by three.

EARLY WHITE BUSH SQUASH.

BOSTON MARROW is a popular variety for Fall and Winter use. With careful treatment it can be kept until the first of January.

The color of the flesh is orange, it is of a fine

SUMMER BUSH CROOKNECK.

grain, and cooks as dry as a Potato. Plant eight by eight.

HUBBARD.—This is a Fall and Winter variety, equal, if not superior, in quality to the Boston Marrow. The skin being very hard, it keeps better; with care it can be kept until May. It is a good variety for garden or field-culture. Plant eight by eight.

YOKOHOMA.—This variety is from Japan, sent here by Mr. Thomas Hogg, and, after a ten years' trial, proves to be a valuable acquisition. It is of a pale green color, changing later in the season to a dull orange. The surface is ribbed and warted. The flesh is solid, orange color, fine grained, and

BOSTON MARROW.

cooks dry, with a high flavor of excellent quality. Can be kept until March.

WINTER CROOKNECK is popular in New England for Winter use. The vines grow luxuriantly and bear a Squash with a long, solid neck; color pale yellow, flesh tender, and good for pies.

Three or four ounces of Squash-seed, of the different kinds, when properly cultivated, will give an abundance for Summer and Winter use.

SWEET POTATO.

*Ipomoea batatas.*

Within the last ten years, the culture of the Sweet Potato has increased very materially, in some of the

Middle States. Formerly the supply for the Northern markets came from Virginia and the Carolinas, but now farmers in New Jersey and other States as far north, having light sandy soil, are turning their attention more and more every year to the cultivation of it as a profitable market crop.

It is useless to attempt growing the Sweet Potatoes, with any hopes of success, on a heavy clay soil. They will only reach their full size on a light, warm, sandy soil. In the Northern or Middle States the plants should be started under glass, and transplanted to the open air in June.

About the first of April a moderate hot-bed is made, putting on top of the manure, when the frame is in place, two inches of good garden-soil. The Potatoes selected for seed, should be fine specimens. These should be cut lengthwise in two, then placed close to each other, flat side down, in the frame, and covered at once with about three inches of garden-mould, putting on the sashes immediately. In fifteen days from the time of planting, the young sprouts will be well above ground; then they should have an abundance of air daily, or else they will grow too long and spindling. They may be grown in hills, three feet apart each way—either in the open field or garden. A shovelful of well-rotted manure is thrown on the spot and well mixed with the soil, forming a raised mound like a Cucumber hill, only larger. The plants may be separated from the Potato by pressing them off with the thumb and finger. They should be at once planted in the hill; this must be done early in June, on a damp or cloudy day.

The ground should be kept free from weeds, by frequent stirrings with a cultivator or hand-hoe. When the vines begin to run, they should be lifted carefully, by hand, and their positions changed, so that they may not take root early in the season. If allowed to do so, the Potatoes, even with a strong growth of vine, will not be as large as they otherwise would.

The Sweet Potato is the only vegetable with which I am familiar that will do better on shallow than on deep-ploughed land. When the ground is worked deep the roots grow long and very slender. In garden-culture, we frequently tramp the spot hard before putting on the manure and making the hill, and find it works well. If the plants are taken off carefully, a second crop of plants will soon come up thickly, and grow full size, in time to set out in the open field. Between three and four thousand plants can be grown under a sash 3 x 6.

When the soil is light and warm, suited to the growth of the Sweet Potato, it is a more profitable crop to raise than the common Potato. From one to two hundred dollars can be made from an acre. Twelve or fifteen hills should yield a bushel of Potatoes.

There are only two or three kinds that are cultivated.

Nansemond is the best and earliest variety grown in the Middle States. The roots are short but thick, flesh yellow, dry, and of a fine flavor.

Yellow Skin is grown chiefly in the Carolinas, where it is highly valued for its fine quality for the table. It grows large, twelve inches long, swollen in the middle, three inches in diameter; flesh yellow and fine grained.

Red Skin.—The roots of this variety grow long and thin. It is not desirable where the other kinds are cultivated.

# CHAPTER XIII.

TOMATO.

*Lycopersicum esculentum.*

THE Tomato is very extensively grown in many sections of the country. When properly managed, it usually pays a handsome profit on the capital invested.

In common with many others, who have been for some years practically engaged in horticultural pursuits, we are frequently questioned by beginners about the cultivation of the Tomato as a source of profit: How much will an acre yield under ordinary treatment, and the sum total that can be relied on with any degree of certainty? It is not an easy matter to answer such queries satisfactorily to the person propounding them, from the fact that so much depends on circumstances, such as proximity to a good market, earliness, and the character of the soil on which they are grown. Even with professional gardeners, the Tomato is a precarious crop. It is exceedingly perishable; three or four days' rain, or damp and muggy weather at the time of ripening, often spoils a very considerable part of the crop; or, even when gathered and packed in good order for market, rough or careless handling will so injure the appearance of Tomatoes, that they have to be sold for a low figure, at a time when sound ones are bringing high rates. Again, a great deal depends upon the skill of the cultivator in preparing his ground and managing his plants, so as to bring the crop forward a week or ten days earlier than the main crop from the same vicinity. We have known of numerous instances where two gardeners in the same neighborhood would grow a certain number of baskets of Tomatoes every year; one of them, by skill and close application to his business, would make from an acre, from five to seven hundred dollars, while the other would not make more than two hundred and fifty dollars. Every intelligent gardener knows the importance, in Tomato culture, of having strong, stout, and stocky plants when the time arrives for transplanting into the open ground. In fact, where this part of the business is overlooked or neglected, it would be wiser and in every way better for the farmer or gardener to devote his land to Potatoes or Corn, instead of Tomatoes.

The consumption of Tomatoes is, of course, immense; but it makes a very decided difference to the grower whether he has a term of one, two, or three weeks in the Tomato season, when his fruit will be in brisk demand at prices ranging from three to four dollars per basket of twenty quarts; or he is compelled to commence selling at fifty cents per basket, on a falling market, which will soon reach ten cents. At these low rates, the demand is not as good as when Tomatoes were bringing three dollars a basket.

Twelve or fourteen days in the date of ripening,

will often make a difference of two or three hundred dollars on an acre. To gain this time, practical gardeners make use of every means to hasten the ripening. Transplanting the plants two or three times before setting them in the field has a tendency to bring about this result, and this system is generally adopted by the best cultivators.

Within the last six or seven years, Tomatoes have been grown in some of the Southern States, and shipped North in such quantities, as to create, what might be termed, a panic among Northern growers. Those sent from points south of Virginia usually arrive in damaged condition, owing to the careless picking and packing of many of the Southern growers, and they have not, so far, conflicted with the interests of Northern gardeners. But Norfolk, Va., and Delaware Tomatoes, are now sent into New York and other Northern markets, almost as fresh as those grown in New Jersey or on Long Island. Large quantities coming from these sources, have reduced the profits of Northern growers.

In growing Tomatoes for market, the frames form a very important but at the same time a very expensive item. At least from six to eight thousand plants can be grown in a seed-bed (full directions for which will be found under Hot-Beds); these, however, must be transplanted into other frames, putting only sixty plants to a sash, and when they are set in place in the field four by four, this would take two thousand seven hundred and twenty-two plants to an acre, and from forty to fifty sashes.

There are hundreds of acres of Tomatoes grown

around New York by contract for canning. For this purpose the matter of earliness is not so important, and a couple of hundred plants may be put in a transplanting bed. The canning companies usually pay from forty to fifty cents a bushel, and growers do well at these prices.

Soil.—The Tomato is one of the few plants grown by market-gardeners for profit that will pay better when planted in a poor than in a rich soil. I do not mean a barren soil, but such as a gardener would look upon as poor. Before planting, the ground should be thoroughly and deeply ploughed and mellowed. Then the furrows should be marked out with two horses and a plough four feet each way. At each intersection throw a small handful of Peruvian guano. Then carefully lift the plants from the frames, each one having a ball or square piece of earth attached to the roots. For this purpose use a long-bladed knife, making a cut on the four sides of the plants, which are then placed in a barrow or spring wagon and taken to the field. The plants are set in place on top of the guano or other stimulant, some soil is drawn around the ball of earth, which is pressed firmly by the hands of the operator, and so on until the field is finished. When the plants have had plenty of room in the frames, then lifted as described above, they are not checked by transplanting in the open ground. The roots will very soon come in contact with the guano; this will force the plants forward more rapidly than any other treatment with which we have experimented. When Tomatoes are planted in strong, rich ground, they run too much to vines; and although, taking the season through, there will be more fruit, it comes too late in the season, when Tomatoes are plenty and cheap.

In cultivating Tomatoes in a large way, the only trouble is to grow the plants. When once in permanent place they require less care than Corn. All that is necessary is to keep the ground well cultivated with horse implements, hand-hoeing once or twice during the season immediately around the plants.

YIELD PER ACRE.—In 1864 we contracted with parties to grow them ten thousand baskets of Tomatoes. The Summer of that year was excessively warm and dry, and from a want of experience in handling and shipping so many, quite a large proportion of them spoiled on the vines. Still, from the number of acres planted, the average yield gathered was nine hundred baskets to the acre. Since then a careful and large grower has assured me that he has repeatedly gathered one thousand bushels from an acre, and I have not the least doubt as to the correctness of the estimate. Taking a small piece of ground, we have frequently got a higher average than this, but when grown by the acre, the calculations have to be made accordingly. It will take about twenty-seven hundred plants to an acre, and each plant should produce one peck of marketable fruit, making about seven hundred bushels.

This is a fair estimate of the yield of Tomatoes, and it can be safely stated that the gardener or farmer, who starts out with a firm determination to cultivate and manage his field with care and discretion may, in a favorable season, rely upon six or seven hundred bushels of Tomatoes to the acre.

These figures are based entirely on good cultivation, for we have seen many an acre of Tomatoes that did not yield two hundred bushels.

Varieties.—There is now a long catalogue of varieties of Tomatoes, many of them recently introduced. Among these new kinds, some have special merit for the kitchen-garden, but so far we have grown no variety that will compare, in earliness, quality, and productiveness for market, with the old favorite.

Smooth Round Red.—It is early, smooth, solid, medium and uniform in size, and ripens to the stem. The best market variety.

Trophy.—This new variety was sent out last Spring for the first time by Col. George E. Waring, of Newport, R. I.

We have cultivated a number of plants of the "Trophy," and we feel satisfied that it is a valuable acquisition to our list of Tomatoes. In quality, quantity of crop, and size of fruit, it is all that Colonel Waring claims for it; in fact, for solidity and quality it is superior to any variety with which we are familiar. Until the time comes when Tomatoes are sold by weight, and not by measure, the Trophy will not become a popular market variety; for the reason that a huckster cannot measure a quart or two of Tomatoes so large as they are. For home consumption, the Trophy cannot help becoming a favorite, provided the variety is kept pure. When it is more generally cultivated, this will be a difficult task. The specimen Tomatoes from which we procured seed were very large, smooth, and round. At least one-half of the crop from this seed was of a different shape, although the whole crop of fruit was of large size. It is not as early as the Smooth Round Red.

TILDEN.—This variety we have grown three years in succession, then dropped it from our list as unworthy of a place. It is a light bearer, not early, and more liable to rot than any of the other large kinds.

COOCK'S FAVORITE.—This is a reliable variety, and popular in some sections for market. The fruit is round, smooth, solid, and abundant. It is not with us as early as the Early Smooth Red.

LESTER'S PERFECTED is large, late; color pinkish red, smooth, and solid. Only fit for home use.

LARGE YELLOW is a medium-sized Tomato, of a bright yellow color. Fruit round and solid. Only grown in the kitchen-garden.

PEAR-SHAPED and CHERRY are grown exclusively for pickling and preserving, for which they are very popular.

Plants for family use can be started, in pots or boxes in warm rooms, in March, and by the middle of May—the time to transplant them—they will be strong and stocky.

Seed may be sown in a protected border in April, and transplanted in June for a late crop, that will yield until frost. The bearing season of all the varieties may be lengthened by training the vines to a frame-work.

From twenty-five to fifty plants will be enough to stock the kitchen-garden, planted four feet apart each way.

### TURNIP.

*Brassica rapa.*

The Turnip crop is an important one to the farmer as well as to the market-gardener. But, as yet, its culture is nothing like as extensive as the value of this root for feeding stock and for culinary purposes would warrant.

In the milk and beef-producing districts of the Middle States, Turnips can be grown with profit for Winter and Spring feeding of stock. Sheep will thrive well when fed in part with Turnips through the cold weather.

We are inclined to believe that the time is not far distant when the good husbandman will be forced to accept this proposition, and devote more acres to the production of this root for stock-feeding.

Within the last dozen years the culture of Turnips has very considerably increased in this country; it will, no doubt, go on steadily from year to year, but more rapidly when farmers will make use of some of the improved horse-tools. These, when properly applied, will reduce the expense of cultivation at least one-half.

The main crop of Turnips is grown in the Fall, and very commonly as a second crop. Those who grow Early Potatoes for market harvest them in time to sow Turnip-seed, and, by this method, produce two crops from the same ground in one year.

In locations where this plan can be carried out, the crop of Turnips will often give as much profit as the crop of Potatoes. We have frequently grown a crop of Strap-leaf Red-Top Turnips on the same ground with Corn, by sowing the seed broadcast in July, just before the Corn was cultivated the last time. We have often had, in this way, three or four hundred bushels of good-sized Turnips in November, from sowing only one pound of seed to the acre.

Soil.—The Turnip will grow freely on any kind of soil—from a light sandy loam, to a heavy clay—provided the ground is mellow and fertile when the seed is sown. This is the important point in growing Turnips. As a matter of course, those kinds that have to be cultivated in rows can be grown with much less expense on a free soil without stones, than on a heavy clay soil with stones. Nor does the soil need to be very rich to produce a full crop. When sown on rich soil, the growth of tops will be too large, without a corresponding growth of the roots.

On ground well manured in the Spring, for Early Potatoes, and after these have been dug, in July, ploughed and harrowed, a crop of Turnips can be grown without any additional manure. But we usually, before harrowing, spread broadcast two or three hundred pounds of superphosphate to the acre. In garden-culture, on ground where Potatoes, Peas, Beans, &c., &c., have been taken off, some wood-ashes, bone-flour, or superphosphate, may be applied in the same way with advantage, before sowing the Turnip-seed.

Culture.—The ground should be well worked

HEXAMER PRONG-HOE.

before sowing the seed. When a Summer crop of Potatoes has been grown, one ploughing, in most instances, will suffice; but, otherwise, two ploughings will be found to give the most satisfactory returns. The time of sowing for the main crop will depend on the location and the kind to be grown. At our farm in New Jersey, we sow the Ruta Baga from the 20th of June until the 15th of July, as the case may be.

With the Yellow Stone, Aberdeen, Long White Cow-Horn, and Strap-leaf Red-Top, we sow them in the order named; in relation to time, from the middle of July to the 1st of September. The last-named sort, which is very extensively grown, will, on well-prepared soil, attain full size in much the shortest time. In 1866 we sowed a field of this kind between the 10th and 15th of September, and in ninety days we gathered a fine crop of Turnips.

In growing Turnips for market or for feeding-purposes, the Ruta Baga is most highly valued. This variety is always grown in rows; in field-culture they should be two feet apart, so as to admit of horse-tools in cultivation. We ridge the ground before sowing the seed, in the same way and for the same reasons as recommended for Carrots. The seed is sown with a machine, using one and a half pounds to an acre. If the seed is fresh and the weather favorable, in twelve days from the date of sowing the plants will be up; then a "root-cleaner" should be run between the rows at once, running twice in each space. This should be repeated in ten or twelve days.

The cost of cultivation is trifling, if the ground between the rows is disturbed often enough to prevent the weeds from starting. "A stitch in time saves nine;" for, if neglected at this stage of growth, the expenses will amount to five times as much, and, at the same time, the crop will be lessened.

When the plants are two or three inches high, they may be thinned out to four inches apart in the row. The thinning can be done more quickly by one person going in advance of the others, with a hoe four inches wide, and chopping out the young Turnips, leaving three or four in a bunch every four inches apart. These are removed by hand, allowing only one to remain in a place. When timely care is taken with Ruta Bagas, this is the only hand-labor called for during their growth. It is frequently recommended to sow the Ruta Baga in seed-beds, and then, at the proper time in favorable weather, transplant into rows at the distances named. We have tried this method time and again, and always with the same result; that is, an increased expense in growing this crop, under our management.

The Yellow Stone and Aberdeen we sow two and three weeks later, treating them in the same way as Ruta Bagas. On very mellow ground we sometimes sow the seed on the level, marking the rows three inches wider, so as to give more room for the horse-tools.

The Cow-Horn and Strap-leaf will yield more to the acre when sown in rows; but, as a rule, farmers sow these two kinds broadcast, because there is no "bother" in cultivation. Last year a friend of the writer raised eight hundred bushels of the Cow-Horn on an acre. The seed was sown broadcast during the first week in August, using only three-quarters of a pound of seed. When sown broadcast and scattered evenly, three-quarters of a pound of fresh seed will be found a full complement for an acre.

In garden-culture, Turnip-seed should always be sown in rows twelve or fifteen inches apart, and the plants thinned to three or four inches apart in the row. For table use, a medium-sized Turnip is preferable.

Two ounces of seed, comprising two or three sorts, will give enough for family use during the Fall, Winter, and Spring.

HARVESTING.—In the latitude of New York, Turnips are pulled in November, by hand, throwing three or four rows together, the roots all one way. The tops are then cut off and the Turnips placed in a root-cellar, or pitted, in the same way as Carrots and Beets. If grown for stock-feeding, the white kinds should be used first. The yellow sorts and Ruta Bagas can be kept, if necessary, until Spring.

## TURNIPS. 249

PROFITS.—These will depend on the locality and the purposes for which Turnips are grown. Where we are located, Ruta Bagas and Yellow Stones are worth, by the quantity, from forty to sixty cents a bushel, and sell readily at these prices. All through the past Winter, Yellow Stones sold for one dollar and seventy-five cents per barrel, and Ruta Bagas for two dollars. At these rates Turnips pay handsomely, when grown as a second crop, with a yield of from four to six hundred bushels to the acre.

VARIETIES.— Of these there can be found a long list on seedsmen's catalogues, but, like most other kinds of vegetables, only a few kinds are grown by those who have experience. Among the best is the

AMERICAN IMPROVED RUTA BAGA.—This variety is cultivated both for market and stock, and is the best on the list.

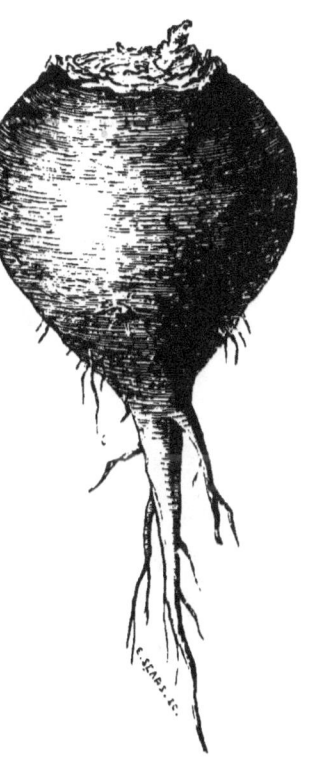

AMERICAN IMPROVED RUTA BAGA.

The flesh is solid, tender, and of delicate flavor when cooked.

LAING'S IMPROVED is a more vigorous grower than the foregoing, and, if on strong ground, the roots will average a third larger in size. They are purple above ground, and yellow below. The flesh is solid and yellow.

Yellow Stone is one of the most profitable and popular varieties that we grow for market or for table use. The root is nearly round, medium-sized, color light yellow. The flesh is yellow and sweet.

Yellow Aberdeen grows to a large size. It is generally grown for feeding cattle; for this object it is a valuable variety.

Cow-Horn.—This kind grows rapidly, forming a long root, not unlike the White Carrot. The Cow-Horn is cultivated exclusively for feeding stock, and when sown in good ground, the yield is very large — from eight hundred to one thousand bushels are frequently produced from an acre.

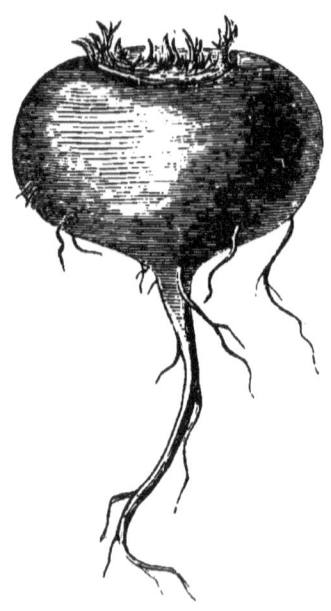

YELLOW STONE.

Strap-leaf Red-Top is well and favorably known in almost every part of the country. It is purple above and white below. The flesh is white, and very tender when cooked (p. 252).

Flat Dutch, or Spring.—The Flat Dutch is sown in the Spring, as an early variety for table use. It is grown on a large scale, by gardeners, in the vicinity of a market.

It is a white Turnip, and when of medium size the quality is good.

Turnips are subject to the ravages of the same kinds of insects that injure Cabbages. We have known instances where the whole crop was badly injured by *club-root*. The black flea (*Haltica striolata*) destroys the young plants when they appear above the surface.

The same remedies recommended for Cabbages will answer for Turnips.

### HERBS.

The vegetable garden is not complete without its stock of the sweet herbs. The treatment of all that are commonly grown is so nearly the same, it is hardly necessary to give separate directions for the various kinds.

A seed-bed should be prepared early in the Spring — made rich, loose, and mellow, raking the surface and removing all stones, lumps, &c., &c. Then open shallow rows one foot apart for the seed. A small package of each kind, costing ten cents, will give an abundance for

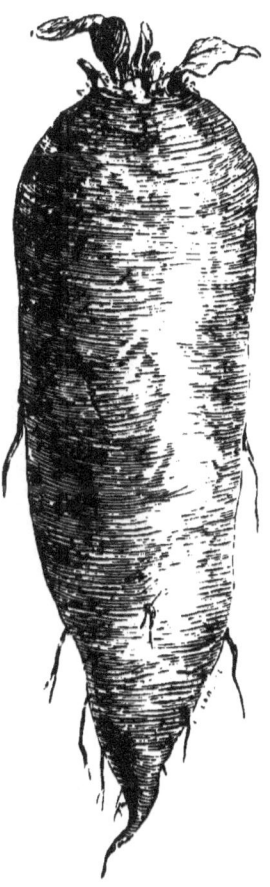

COW-HORN.

family use. The seed is sown in these drills, each kind by itself, and covered by raking the bed in the direction of the rows. The seed-bed should be kept free from weeds by frequent disturbance of the soil. When the plants are an inch above the surface, they may be thinned out to four inches apart in the row.

STRAP-LEAF RED-TOP.

A larger yield will be obtained by transplanting into another bed in June, setting the plants one foot apart each way. The only care will be to prevent the weeds from gaining any headway.

In the Fall, the tops should be cut off, tied in

small bunches, dried, and then carefully packed away in boxes until wanted.

Among those in general use, may be named Basil, Caraway, Marjoram, Rose Mary, Sage, Summer Savory, and Thyme.

# CHAPTER XIV.

### FORCING-HOUSES FOR VEGETABLES.

The culture of special crops, on an extensive scale, is now the policy of the most successful gardeners around New York, and the tendency of the entire trade is gradually working in the same direction.

For many years past there has been, in New York and Boston, a large and growing demand, during the Winter and Spring months, for what gardeners call, *Frame Lettuce*. As managed at present, with bottom-heat, growing this kind of Lettuce is a large, and, when properly understood, a lucrative branch of gardening.

Until recently, this Winter Lettuce was brought forward in hot-beds, started in the Fall. If found necessary, the manure was renewed during the Winter, after the first or second crop had been sold, so that three crops of Lettuce and one of Cucumbers were, with close attention, taken off from these *beds* between the first of November and the fifteenth of June.

Within the last three years a number of forcing-houses, heated by hot water, have been built in the vicinity of New York, by gardeners, for the purpose of growing vegetables (Lettuce, Radishes, and Cucumbers), during the Winter. Some of these houses in our neighborhood, have now been in operation two years. We have watched their workings with a considerable degree of interest, and we have concluded that this style of structure, for the purpose named, is more economical, and for those who can command the means requisite for building, it will eventually supersede the old hot-bed system. With one of these houses, a private family

RIDGE-POLE.

could have the table well supplied, at a comparatively trifling cost, with fresh vegetables through the whole Winter; besides such a building could, at any time, be turned into a green-house or conservatory.

With the commercial gardener, this is a new branch of the business, and many mistakes will probably be made at the outset, both in construction and in management, while the crops are growing, by allowing the temperature to be regulated by inexperienced persons. When forcing Lettuce or Radishes, the temperature, during the cold weather, should be through the night about forty-five degrees, and during the day not above seventy degrees—ranging between these two figures.

These houses may be built any desired length from one to three hundred feet and from two to eight in width, or connected, as shown in the end view, p. 255.

Each house is eleven feet wide, with a table on either side and a passage-way twenty inches wide, the floor of which should be six and a half feet clear from the ridge-pole.

These buildings are heated by hot water, a double row of four-inch pipes, under each table, supported every ten or twelve feet by brick pillars, eighteen inches high, which will bring the pipes within fifteen inches of the tables.

There are quite a number of these patent heating apparatuses, now in general use, near New York. As far as we have been able to examine them, there is very little difference, either in the expense or in the working of some of these various patents. Of those most popular among gardeners, are Hichings & Co's., C. R. Ellis's, and Weathered and Chesevoy's any one of which will answer the purpose.

The outside walls should be put up as follows: a post is set every four feet and weather-boarded, then a space on the inside of two inches, and an eight-inch brick wall, on which rests the outside gutter plate.

The ridge-pole is five inches by two and a half, cut in on either side three-quarters of an inch (as seen on p. 255), to give a bearing for the upper end of the sash to rest on. The gutter plates are twelve inches wide, four inches thick, and supported by posts every ten or twelve feet. A narrow board is nailed inside, on each side of the plate, for the lower end of the sash to rest on. The sashes are 3 x 6 and made of glass 8 x 10, on account of giving more light. Every alternate sash is permanently fastened by three large screws on either end. The others can be raised up on top to admit air, when necessary. This is conveniently done by having a piece of flat iron fastened to the sash, and three or four holes in the iron. The sash is raised to the height required, by this piece of iron and secured by a pin driven in the ridge-pole, which holds the iron in place.

On the inside of the lower end of the frame of each of the movable sashes, is screwed a piece of inch stuff, three and a half feet long. Two inches of this narrow strip of wood, on either side, will project under the permanent sashes and thus prevent the movable ones from being lifted off by a gale of wind. All through the Winter, and more especially towards Spring, a considerable amount of water is needed to keep the plants in good condition. This water is saved from the gutters of the houses, led by pipes into a cistern, which runs across the houses. A neighbor who has three houses, one hundred and twenty feet long, each, has a cistern, twenty-seven feet long, eight feet deep and seven feet wide, which holds a sufficient supply of water. Another grower, who has five connected houses, each two hundred feet long, has a different arrangement. At about one hundred feet from either end of these houses, the pitch of the roof is changed, running across from east to west, the main houses run from north to south. This is intended for economy in time, in being able to go from one house to another, without having to go to either end. At the west end of this cross-pitch is a one-quarter horse-power Ericsson's caloric engine, attached to a small pump, throwing an inch stream. Above this apparatus there is a tank, made of two-inch chestnut and lined with lead. Around this tank, which holds four hundred gallons, there is a brick wall, leaving a space of three or four inches between the outside of the tank and the bricks.

In less than two hours, and with an expense of about eight or ten pounds of coal, this little engine fills the tank with water.

ERICSSON'S CALORIC ENGINE AND PUMP.

The hose, one and a quarter inches, for watering, is attached to the tank, and by this means one man or boy can water the beds, instead of two, which the hand force-pump requires. The total cost of this engine and pump is two hundred and fifty dollars—it more than pays for itself in a year. The caloric engine needs no engineer to attend to it; there is no danger of an explosion, and it does the work of pumping this daily amount of water at very low cost.

At the southern end of these houses, every inch of space is utilized, and economically laid out, by continuing the glass roof around the end, leaving a passage-way inside connecting all the five houses, with a forcing-table on either side of this passage.

A shed made of wood or brick is necessary at the north end of the houses. This will serve a double purpose—as a market-house for preparing the "stuff," and it will prevent the snow from drifting into the alleys. A board fence running along the west side, will also be found of service for this purpose.

The tables should be three or four inches below the lower edge of the gutter plates, to prevent rotting of the timbers. All the boards of the tables should be painted with tar, before putting them in place. There is nothing gained by boarding up the sides, along the passage-way—a single board five or six inches wide, nailed along the outside edge to keep the earth in its place, will be quite sufficient.

A rich soil, about six or seven inches deep, made up of one-third well-rotted manure and two-thirds garden soil is put on the tables. The first crop of Lettuce, thirty-five plants to a sash is planted about the 20th of October. Very little heat is required before December. This crop is ready for market about Christmas. The soil is then worked over and planted again. This crop will be ready in about nine weeks more—then a third planting is set out, to be followed by cucumbers.

At first, gardeners depended on plants grown in the Fall, for the several crops, but during last Winter, a few, who fell short of old plants, sowed seed in the houses at the time of planting the Lettuce.

These plants were large enough for the next crop, and did much better than the older ones.

It will take about four tons of coal to heat one hundred feet of house, and one boiler will heat three hundred feet with twelve tons.

The total expense of building this kind of house will average from ten dollars to thirteen dollars a foot, according to circumstances. This includes not only the houses, but all the forcing-pumps, &c., &c.

The gross receipts from the four crops, will amount to about five dollars a sash; from which two dollars may be deducted for expenses, leaving a profit of three dollars a sash. We have known frequently of profits being double this amount, but some instances have also come under our notice where they were not as large.

A crop of Radishes will pay about the same as Lettuce, per sash—the only advantage is, that Radishes will be ready for market in six or seven weeks, while Lettuce will take nine.

James Muir & Sons, who have seven hundred and eighty feet of this class of forcing-houses, which cost them for construction ten dollars a lineal foot, now, after two years' experience, make the following exhibit of one year's crops:

| | |
|---|---|
| Gross receipts from four crops | $2,562 41 |
| Interest on $7,800, at 10 per cent. | $780 00 |
| Coal | 200 00 |
| Labor | 300 00 |
| Manure | 50 00 |
| | 1,330 00 |
| Net profits | $1,232 41 |

Let no one flatter himself that this business is all 'sunshine.' There are serious obstacles constantly presenting themselves, very discouraging to those who have already built this kind of house for forcing vegetables. The greatest drawback is the *damping off* of the plants in some parts of the beds. This occurs at any stage of the growth, and without any apparent cause. Sometimes when the Lettuce is half or two-thirds grown, in certain spots, the plants look wilted, the leaves droop, and they might just as well be pulled out at once and thrown away, for they only get worse the longer they remain. A friend, who is largely engaged in this business, told me a short time ago, that in one of his houses at least a third of the crop was worthless from this cause, while in the other two houses along side, planted and cared for in the same way, there was not an injured specimen to be found. In some cases the roots are rotted off, in others the outside coating of the root seems loose and comes off very readily, no insect marks of any kind being discernible in either instance. Again, the roots may be sound, but the leaves lose vigor and droop when the sun shines. I am inclined to think that this condition or disease is brought about by keeping the temperature of the houses above fifty degrees with fire-heat.

The *aphides*, or "green fly," are very troublesome; if neglected they will soon get the better of the gardener and destroy his crop of Lettuce in part or entirely. They are very destructive, and multiply at an enormous rate. To guard against these little pests the houses must be fumigated with Tobacco stems twice a week. For this purpose a number of sheet-iron furnaces, about fifteen inches high and eight in diameter, with a grate placed near the bottom, and an opening below to give draft, are very serviceable. Some shavings and Tobacco stems are put into the furnaces, which are placed in different parts of the houses, then lighted, and the work is very soon accomplished. To prevent the Tobacco from burning too fast a cover is placed on each furnace; this checks the draft and increases the quantity of smoke.

As stated in the chapter on Hot-Beds, the curled varieties of Lettuce will not answer for forcing. The most reliable kinds for this purpose are the Tennis Ball and Boston Head, or White-seeded Butter Lettuce.

In planting three or four houses with Lettuce it is advisable not to plant the whole at the same time; it will be better to have some difference in the date of ripening.

The space under the tables can be used in growing Rhubarb, for which there is a demand, early in the season, at high prices. Chives can also be forced in the same way, or, better still, they can be put into thumb-pots and set on the ground under the tables.

Asparagus can be forced in these houses, with more economy than in hot-beds, from roots five or six years old. Also, Strawberries will do well, if planted on the tables, at any time during the Winter, eight inches apart each way. In conclusion, any kind of "stuff" that can be grown in a hot-bed or green-house, can also be grown in these forcing-houses.

# CHAPTER XV.

#### A LIST OF VEGETABLE SEEDS FOR THE KITCHEN-GARDEN.

For those persons who are not familiar with the best kinds and quantity of garden Seed necessary to supply a family of eight or ten persons, I append the following list, which may help beginners, or those who may want to stock their gardens with an abundant supply of the leading kinds of vegetables for home use. With Radishes, Peas, and Bush Beans, there should be a succession of plantings, say every two or three weeks, from April until the middle of July. This will give a supply of young Radishes, Peas, and Beans until late in the Fall.

#### DWARF BEANS.

Early Valentine, Refugee or One Thousand to One, and White Kidney; two quarts of the three sorts.

#### POLE BEANS.

Large White Lima, and Horticultural Cranberry; one pint each, will plant one hundred and fifty hills.

#### BEETS.

Early Blood Turnip, Bassano, and Long Smooth Blood; two ounces of each.

#### CABBAGE.

Jersey Wakefield for early, Large Flat Dutch and Drumhead Savoy for late. A small package of each kind, or one hundred plants of each sort, will be an abundance.

#### SWEET CORN.

Two quarts of a couple or three varieties, planted at different dates, will be enough.

#### CUCUMBER.

White Spine and Long Green; one ounce of each will be enough for early and late.

#### CARROT.

Long Orange, or Bliss' Improved Long Orange, are the best varieties for the garden; two ounces of either will be enough.

#### CAULIFLOWER.

Half Early Paris, and Early Erfurt, are the most reliable; half an ounce of either will give plenty of plants.

#### CELERY.

White Solid, Dwarf Incomparable, or Boston Market; one ounce will give three thousand plants.

#### EGG PLANT.

The Improved New York is the best. A small paper of seed will give enough of plants. When they grow well, they will produce from six to ten eggs to a plant—twenty-five plants.

### LETTUCE.

Simpson's Curled and Black Seeded Butter; a small paper of each.

### MUSK MELON.

Skillman's Fine Netted, and Nutmeg; one ounce will plant fifty hills.

### WATER MELON.

Mountain Sweet and Mountain Sprout (and Citron for preserves); one ounce will plant thirty hills.

### ONIONS.

Wethersfield Large Red, Yellow Danvers, and White Portugal; four ounces of seed will produce enough for table use.

### PARSNIPS.

Long Smooth; one ounce of fresh seed.

### PEAS.

Philadelphia Extra Early, Tom Thumb, Champion of England, White and Black Marrowfats; one pint of each, sowed in the order named.

### PEPPERS.

Large Squash and Bull-Nose; a small paper of seed will give plants enough—twenty-five plants.

### RADISH.

Early Turnip Scarlet, Short-Top Long Scarlet, White Spanish, Black Spanish; one ounce of each, sowed in the order named.

### SPINACH.

Round Smooth-leaved; four ounces sowed in September and two in April.

### SALSIFY.

This vegetable should be included in every well-stocked garden; two ounces will be enough.

### SQUASH.

White Bush, White Summer Crook Neck, Boston Marrow, and Hubbard; one ounce of the early varieties will plant forty hills, and the same quantity of seed will plant only twenty hills of the Boston Marrow or Hubbard.

### TOMATO.

Smooth Round Red and Trophy, a small paper of each, or fifty plants, will give an abundant supply.

### TURNIPS.

White Dutch, (for early), Strap-leaf Red-Top, Yellow Stone, and Improved American Ruta Baga: one ounce of each.

## A LIST OF SEEDS.

### THE QUANTITY OF SEED TO AN ACRE.

| | |
|---|---|
| Beans (bush, | 1½ bush. |
| " Pole, | 12 qts. |
| Beets, | 5 lbs. |
| Carrots, | 4 " |
| Cucumbers, | 2 " |
| Corn (in hills), | 8 qts. |
| Musk Melon, | 2 lbs. |
| Water " | 3 to 4 lbs. |
| Onions, | 4 to 5 " |
| Parsnips, | 4 " |
| Peas (in drills), | 1½ bush, |
| Radishes, | 5 lbs. |
| Salsify, | 5 " |
| Spinach, | 6 " |
| Squash, | 3 " |
| Turnips in drills, | 1½ " |
| " broadcast, | 1 " |

The quantities given are often varied. In case we have any doubts about the seed being fresh, the quantity is increased, &c. &c.

### VITALITY OF GARDEN SEED.

The vitality of many kinds of garden seeds will depend on the temperature in which they are kept. As fast as the different kinds of such are gathered, properly dried and cleaned in the Summer and Fall, they should be put in cotton bags, and tied up to the rafters in the seed-room or garret, where the dry air can circulate about them freely. When stored in a damp, close atmosphere, garden seeds will very soon lose their germinating power.

As a rule fresh seed are best, but there are a number of kinds that are just as good at three or four years old as they were at one.

Asparagus and Beets are good at two years. Carrot, Egg Plant, Parsnip, Salsify, Onion, Peas and Beans, should always be of the previous year's growth. Cabbage-seed, is good for five years. Celery, Parsley, Spinach, Turnip, Radishes, Cauliflower and Lettuce, are good for two years. Cucumbers, Melons, Squash, and Pumpkins, are better at six years than one.

### DISTANCE TABLE.

The following table will be found useful in calculating the number of plants that can be set on an acre, also for the distribution of manure, laying out beds, &c. &c.

There are forty-three thousand five hundred and sixty square feet in an acre of ground, and when set at the respective distance apart, will contain the numbers designated.

| Distance. | | Number. | Distance. | | Number. |
|---|---|---|---|---|---|
| 1 ft. by | 1 ft. | 43,560 | 6 ft. by 6 ft. | | 1,210 |
| 1½ " | 1½ | 19,360 | 9 " | 9 | 537 |
| 2 " | 2 | 10,890 | 12 " | 12 | 302 |
| 2½ " | 2½ | 6,970 | 15 " | 15 | 194 |
| 3 " | 1 | 14,520 | 18 " | 18 | 134 |
| 3 " | 2 | 7,260 | 20 " | 20 | 103 |
| 3 " | 3 | 4,840 | 25 " | 25 | 70 |
| 4 " | 4 | 2,722 | 30 " | 30 | 40 |
| 5 " | 5 | 1,742 | 40 " | 40 | 27 |

www.ingramcontent.com/pod-product-compliance
Lightning Source LLC
Chambersburg PA
CBHW032143230426
43672CB00011B/2439